SOUTHERN ONTARIO'S
NATIONAL PARKS

SOUTHERN ONTARIO'S
NATIONAL PARKS

N. GLENN PERRETT

FITZHENRY & WHITESIDE

Copyright © 2019 N. Glenn Perrett
Published in Canada by Fitzhenry & Whiteside,
195 Allstate Parkway, Markham, ON   L3R 4T8
Published in the United States by Fitzhenry & Whiteside
311 Washington Street, Brighton, MA   02135

All rights reserved. No part of this book may be reproduced in any manner without the express written consent of the publisher, except in the case of brief excerpts in critical reviews and articles. All inquiries should be addressed to Fitzhenry & Whiteside, 195 Allstate Parkway, Markham, ON   L3R 4T8
2 4 6 8 10 9 7 5 3 1
Library and Archives Canada Cataloguing in Publication

Perrett, N. Glenn, 1960-, author
"Southern Ontario's National Parks / N. Glenn Perrett. — First edition.

Includes index.
ISBN 978-1-55455-397-6 (softcover)

1. National parks and reserves—Ontario, Southern—Guidebooks.
2. Ontario, Southern—Guidebooks.   I. Title.

FC3063.G54 2018   917.1304′5   C2018-901885-2

Publisher Cataloging-in-Publication Data (U.S.)

Names: Perrett, N. Glenn, author.
Title: Southern Ontario's National Parks / author, N. Glenn Perrett.
Description: Markham, Ontario : Fitzhenry & Whiteside Limited, 2019. | Includes bibliographical references and index.
|Summary: "An illustrated guidebook and travel companion to the National Parks of Canada found in Southern Ontario which explores the animals, plants, ecosystems, environment, history, nature, marine life, biology, hiking trails and canoe and kayaking routes within" – Provided by publisher.
Identifiers: ISBN 978-1-55455-397-6 (paperback)
Subjects: LCSH: National parks and reserves – Canada. | Ontario, Southern – Description and travel. | BISAC: TRAVEL / Canada / Ontario (ON).
Classification: LCC F1011.P477 | DDC 917.13 – dc23

Fitzhenry & Whiteside acknowledges with thanks the Canada Council for the Arts and the Ontario Arts Council for their support of our publishing program.
We acknowledge the financial support of the Government of Canada through the Canada Book Fund (CBF) for our publishing activities.

Unless otherwise noted, all photographs by Lynn and N. Glenn Perrett.
Design by Kerry Designs
Printed in Canada by Marquis

For Gleannan and Liam.
May wilderness always enrich your lives.

CONTENTS

1. INTRODUCTION
Page 1

2. BRUCE PENINSULA NATIONAL PARK
Page 11

3. FATHOM FIVE NATIONAL MARINE PARK
Page 47

4. GEORGIAN BAY ISLANDS NATIONAL PARK
Page 73

5. POINT PELEE NATIONAL PARK
Page 105

6. ROUGE NATIONAL URBAN PARK
Page 137

7. THOUSAND ISLANDS NATIONAL PARK
Page 161

8. HEALTHY ENCOUNTERS: NATURE'S MANY BENEFITS
Page **195**

PARK ETIQUETTE, SAFETY AND MINIMAL FOOTPRINTS
Page **204**

9. A FINAL WORD
Page **209**

ENDNOTES
Page **215**

SELECT BIBLIOGRAPHY
Page **217**

ACKNOWLEDGEMENTS
Page **219**

ABOUT THE AUTHOR
Page **221**

DISCLAIMER
Page **223**

Spectacular rugged coastline in Bruce Peninsula National Park

1. INTRODUCTION

"In wildness is the preservation of the world." – Henry David Thoreau

Those of us who reside in Ontario are fortunate to live in close proximity to a wide selection of parks, conservation areas, trails and other green spaces – including wetlands. In fact, Ontario has approximately a quarter of Canada's wetlands and as much as 6% of the world's wetlands. While we haven't been very good stewards of these special habitats, when it comes to wetlands Ontarians are still very rich indeed.

Here in Southern Ontario we are also blessed with six spectacular *national* parks. Unfortunately, most of us are not aware of just how lucky we are to have so many national parks close by because most of us would be hard pressed to name them– and no, Algonquin Park is not a national park, it's Algonquin *Provincial* Park.

One of the first things that I became aware of when I wrote my book *Hikes & Outings of South-Central Ontario* was just how many fascinating wilderness areas exist practically in our backyard. There are dozens within a 30-minute drive of our home in Mulmur, and many more if I travel only a little farther. I also learned that my ignorance of the wilderness bounty that exists in Southern and Central Ontario is shared by many others – even those

Honeymoon Bay, Georgian Bay Islands National Park

who enjoy camping, hiking, kayaking and canoeing. I was soon to realize that my lack of knowledge about nearby national parks was likewise lacking (at least I am consistent.)

Many years ago I was asked to write an article on Georgian Bay Islands National Park. Even though our family has had a cottage on Georgian Bay since the 1960s, and it isn't too far from the park, I never knew that the park existed. I was further surprised to learn that here, in Southern Ontario, you don't have to travel far to find a national park.

In Southwestern Ontario, for instance, lies Point Pelee National Park — a park located not too far from where I spent seven years of my childhood in Sarnia.

Located a little over a two-hour drive from our current home are two national parks situated at the tip of the Bruce Peninsula. Bruce Peninsula National Park is a large park and next to it is the smaller Fathom Five National Marine Park. While I have heard nice things about the Bruce Peninsula over the years, I had never visited the area until I started this book. Now "the Bruce" is a place that my wife Lynn and I keep returning to over and over.

Situated a short distance from where I grew up in Thornhill in the 1970s and early 1980s is Rouge National Urban Park. Extending from Lake Ontario in the south to the Township of Uxbridge in the north, this urban park is 22 times larger than Central Park in New York

Flowerpot Island is a popular site in Fathom Five National Marine Park

Fall in Rouge National Urban Park

and is located, yes, right in the Greater Toronto Area (GTA).

The southeastern part of the province is well-represented as well, with the spectacular Thousand Islands National Park, a real gem covering a stretch of mainland and islands in the historic St. Lawrence River.

The six national parks in Southern Ontario contain exceptional pockets of remaining wilderness located within this densely populated, largely developed part of the country. Point Pelee National Park offers an incredible marsh and beaches along with rare Carolinian forest. Bruce Peninsula National Park features lakes, incredible trails, large, intact forest habitat, scenic cliffs and an ancient cliff-face forest. Fathom Five National Marine Park protects many shipwrecks, historical lighthouses and scenic islands, including the famous Flowerpot Island. Georgian Bay Islands National Park comes with a rich history, featuring Beausoleil Island and a stretch of other beautiful park islands that are part of the Thirty Thousand Islands – the planet's largest freshwater archipelago. The trail system and camping opportunities on Beausoleil are excellent, as is the boating in this water access park. Rouge National Urban Park, Canada's first national urban park, protects several important watersheds while providing a variety of local wilderness opportunities to approximately one-fifth of the country's population – who can get here by public transit. Thousand Islands

The cottage on Georgian Bay where the author spent many summers

National Park is a beauty, offering hiking, camping, boating, kayaking and canoeing not far from what was once the capital of the United Province of Canada — Kingston.

Each of these parks is a special place offering a variety of wonderful wilderness experiences where you can reconnect with nature.

Our family lives between Orangeville and Collingwood and we are able to enjoy day trips to all of these parks. Granted, some are a four-hour drive away, but that still leaves much of the day to enjoy several activities, provided that we get an early start. Certainly spending a few days, or even a week, would be preferable, but each park is definitely worth visiting — even if you only have a day to spare.

While each park is quite different, they all feature remarkable terrestrial and aquatic habitats. In fact, water is a large part of each park. And as Wallace J. Nichols noted in his book *Blue Mind: The Surprising Science That Shows How Being Near, In, On, or Under Water Can Make You Happier, Healthier, More Connected, and Better at What You Do,* our relationship with water can aid us in various ways, including physically, cognitively, healthfully, creatively and spiritually.

Just getting out and experiencing nature is healthful in itself. Unfortunately today, many children and adults spend little time in the natural world thereby missing out on Mother Nature's many benefits. Richard Louv, author of *Last Child in the Woods,* referred to this as "nature-deficit disorder." This is not a good thing as a long walk in the woods can reduce stress and symptoms related to attention disorders, help with depression as well as improve healing. Of course getting out and experiencing nature also involves physical exercise which has shown to help with obesity, heart disease and diabetes.

The six parks in this book offer numerous ways to enjoy the wilderness protected within their boundaries. But before heading out, take time to plan your nature outing. Gathering information about the park you plan on visiting

Point Pelee National Park

Thousand Islands area

is not only a fun way to prepare for your trip, it can help ensure that your visit goes safely and as planned. You can readily obtain further information from the park's websites and by contacting the parks for visitor guides and other informative literature available to the public.

Becoming familiar with park regulations is important. Park wardens are responsible for the national parks by enforcing the *Canada National Parks Act,* the *Criminal Code* as well as provincial laws. Knowing what you can and can't do regarding things like wildlife viewing, noise, fire, camping, boating, animal companions and other topics can save you from being charged with an offence. Some national park offences can result in significant fines and even jail time. Knowing that it is illegal to feed or entice wild animals in a national park or to collect plants, fossils or natural objects can save you from committing an illegal act.

In this book you will find information on park history, habitats, geology, flora and fauna as well as activities within each park featured. I have also included some of our personal adventures at different times of year. We have visited both Point Pelee National Park and Thousand Islands National Park twice and have enjoyed each of the other national parks in this book on numerous occasions. I have intentionally avoided including park information that is likely to change on a regular basis and which is easily obtained from the park's website and social media sites.

Complementing the chapters are pieces on the importance of nature, safety and park etiquette as well as an evaluation of the parks and the park experience.

Enjoy the parks!
N. Glenn Perrett
Mulmur, Ontario

PARK WEBSITES

Bruce Peninsula National Park   www.parkscanada.gc.ca/bruce
Fathom Five National Marine Park   www.parkscanada.gc.ca/fathomfive
Georgian Bay Islands National Park   www.parkscanada.gc.ca/gbi
Point Pelee National Park   www.parkscanada.gc.ca/pelee
Rouge National Urban Park   www.parkscanada.gc.ca/rouge
Thousand Islands National Park   www.parkscanada.gc.ca/ti

Bob Hunter Memorial Park, Rouge National Urban Park   Photo: © Gleannan Perrett

Experiencing nature is a healthy activity

Boulder Beach provides spectacular views of Georgian Bay and is a good spot to watch waves on a windy day

2. BRUCE PENINSULA NATIONAL PARK

"In the woods a man casts off his years, as the snake his slough, and at what period soever of life, is always a child." – Ralph Waldo Emerson

When you visit Bruce Peninsula National Park (BPNP) you will be greeted by spectacular cliffs, scenic shorelines, ancient forests, rare limestone barrens, hiking trails, beaches, lakes, wetlands – and much more. Established in 1987 and located at the tip of the Bruce Peninsula, this more than 150-square-kilometre park contains a variety of habitat types that are home to numerous species of plants and animals.

One of the objectives in creating Canada's 33rd national park was to protect a representative example of the St. Lawrence Lowlands natural region – a narrow area consisting of flat to gently rolling land that extends from Windsor to Quebec City. A few years after creation of the park, the United Nations Educational, Scientific, and Cultural Organization (UNESCO) designated the Niagara Escarpment a Biosphere Reserve with Bruce Peninsula National Park being a core protected area. The "Biosphere Reserve" designation is given to internationally significant

> **BRUCE PENINSULA NATIONAL PARK**
> - Numerous lakes, incredible trails, large, intact forest habitat, scenic cliffs
> - Ancient cliff-face forest
> - Rare alvar habitat
> - More than 40 species of orchids

THE BRUCE TRAIL

The unique qualities of the Niagara Escarpment were recognized by the United Nations Educational, Scientific, and Cultural Organization (UNESCO) in 1990 when it designated the Escarpment as a Biosphere Reserve. Thirty years earlier, in 1959, the exceptional nature of this spectacular landform was recognized by Ray Lowes who had the idea of creating a hiking trail along the length of the Escarpment in Ontario. The Bruce Trail Committee held its first meeting in 1960 and in 1962 Philip Gosling became the first Trail Director, leading the planning and blazing of the trail.

To make this nature trail a reality, the Bruce Trail Conservancy (BTC) worked together with Escarpment landowners to allow people to hike from Queenston to Tobermory. The trail opened officially in 1967. Today the Bruce Trail consists of approximately 900 kilometres of main trail with more than 400 kilometres of side trails making it the oldest and longest continuous footpath in Canada.

The mission of the BTC, a charitable organization, is to establish and maintain a conservation corridor with a public trail to both protect natural areas along the corridor and provide public access. Ecosystems protected along the Bruce Trail include wetlands, forests, meadows and cliffs.

Protecting this nature corridor along the Escarpment is not only beneficial to people, it's vital to other species. The long, unfragmented wilderness passage gives species a protected, natural travel corridor in a rapidly developing part of the province. Such habitat corridors also provide more foraging areas and shelter, increased migration between

Cairn in Tobermory's harbour marking the northern terminus of the Bruce Trail

While the BTC has done an impressive job working with landowners to ensure public access, the trail is not secure unless the land it goes through is secure. To this end the BTC accepts land donations and purchases land as well. Currently, approximately 60% of the wilderness corridor is secure with the BTC having preserved more than 4,000 hectares of Escarpment land.

Some of the most rugged and scenic parts of the Bruce Trail run through Bruce Peninsula National Park. This section of trail is overseen by the Peninsula Bruce Trail Club (PBTC) – one of nine member clubs of the Bruce Trail Conservancy. The PBTC is responsible for more than 240 kilometres of Bruce Trail, from Wiarton to Tobermory.

For more information:
Bruce Trail Conservancy http://brucetrail.org
Peninsula Bruce Trail Club www.pbtc.ca

Bruce Peninsula National Park features rugged coastlines

ecosystems, such as the Galapagos Islands and Africa's Serengeti, and promotes protection and sustainable use.

Bruce Peninsula National Park is also part of the Niagara Escarpment Parks and Open Space System (NEPOSS), a network of many parks and open spaces that protect unique ecological areas, provide outdoor recreation opportunities and secure a route for the Bruce Trail. And it is within BPNP where you'll find some of the most challenging and scenic locations on the Bruce Trail.

There is lots to do at Bruce Peninsula National Park. Its many interior lakes and scenic, rugged coastlines make it ideal for sightseers and photographers. Hikers will enjoy the many trails within the park including approximately 23 kilometres of main track of the famous Bruce Trail. Canoeing and kayaking are also permitted. You can paddle Cyprus Lake which leads into Cameron Lake. There are also good locations to go swimming, especially on Cyprus Lake and the scenic sandy shoreline found at Singing Sands beach at Dorcas Bay on Lake Huron. There are many easily accessible picnic areas within the park as well. There is even a location where you can do some "bouldering," a form of rock climbing without use of ropes or harnesses.

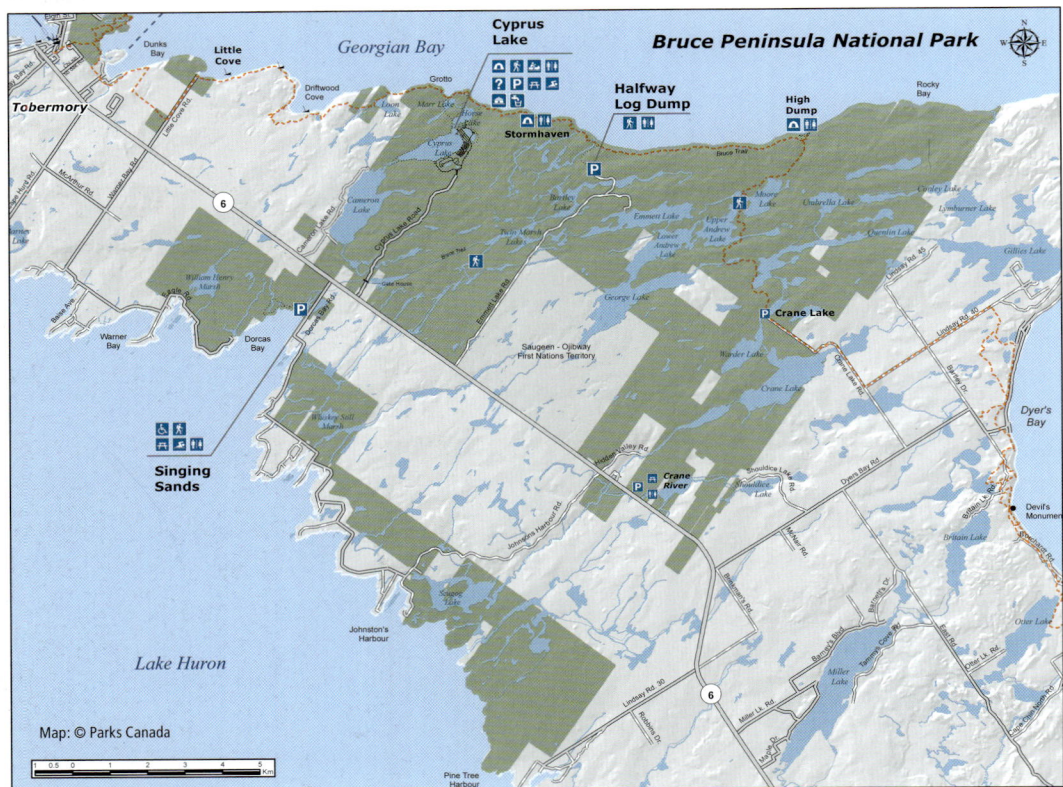

These and other activities await you at Bruce Peninsula National Park.

PARK HISTORY

Although Bruce Peninsula National Park was officially established on July 20, 1987, the area's potential as a national park was seen more than four decades earlier when, in the 1940s, a Member of Parliament proposed that a national park be established on the Bruce Peninsula.[1]

Public consultation was an important part in establishing this national park. And it all began in 1981 when Bob Day, who was Superintendent of Georgian Bay Islands National Park, began to coordinate this important, and controversial, task. The proposed park site overlapped two townships – St. Edmunds and Lindsay. While St. Edmunds supported the park proposal, Lindsay Township did not, so lands in that township were removed from the proposal. On January 1, 1999 Bruce Peninsula National Park became part of the Municipality of Northern Bruce Peninsula. This new township was an amalgamation of the townships of St. Edmunds, Lindsay and Eastnor as well as the village of Lion's Head.

The park is approximately 156 square

kilometres in size. The Province of Ontario transferred thousands of hectares for the new park to the Government of Canada when they signed a Federal-Provincial Agreement on July 20, 1987. This agreement established both the Bruce Peninsula National Park and Fathom Five National Marine Park. Cyprus Lake Provincial Park was one piece of property that the province gave to BPNP under the Federal-Provincial Agreement.

Although the park is relatively young, its human history dates back quite a way. Archaeological evidence indicates that the Saugeen Ojibway Nation has lived in this area for thousands of years.

While humans have existed for millennia in this area and the Odawa and Ojibway were here in the 1600s when the first European explorers arrived, it was European settlement in the 1800s that has had a lasting effect on the park area and its environs. With huge demand for lumber and much of Ontario already depleted of trees, lumber barons set their sights on St. Edmunds Township as early as 1870.

The lumber trade was the first major industry to arrive in St. Edmunds Township and it did well here from the early 1870s until the early 1900s providing settlers with much paid work. The efficiency with which the trees were removed and the subsequent impact on the area is well captured in the book *Hewers of the Forests Fishers of the Lakes: A History of Tobermory and St. Edmunds Township 1870 – 1984*.

Cedars grow on the cliffs in the park

"By 1910, the timbering industry in St. Edmunds had definitely come to the end of its big boom. The rapid removal of trees practiced by the timbermen had practically denuded many areas of St. Edmunds. Brush fires were responsible for destroying a large part of what the timbermen had left behind. With the decline of timbering, St. Edmunds slipped into an economic lull that endured until the tourism industry took hold."

Despite the fact that the lumber boom was over by the early 1900s, logging continued on a smaller scale. The extensive logging, along

Trails can be challenging in winter

Another attraction established in the 1960s was Cyprus Lake Provincial Park. This scenic area, which was transferred to the federal government in 1987 to become a part of Bruce Peninsula National Park, includes a campground as well as Cyprus Lake, Horse Lake, Marr Lake and some of Georgian Bay's spectacular, rugged coastline.

Today Bruce Peninsula National Park is responsible for much of the area's tourism as it attracts hundreds of thousands of visitors to the park annually to camp, hike, swim, canoe, picnic and just take in the spectacular scenery, including popular places such as the Grotto, Singing Sands, Little Cove and Cyprus Lake.

HABITATS

with fires and agriculture, decimated the majority of forests, including those that would later become Bruce Peninsula National Park.

As the lumber industry ground to a halt, tourism became increasingly important on the peninsula. Tourists from the south have enjoyed Tobermory and its scenic surroundings since the early twentieth century with cottages and shops appearing along the rugged shores not long after.

The 1960s saw the creation of the Bruce Trail, which officially opened in 1967. At nearly 900 kilometres, the trail is the longest continuous footpath in Canada and runs along the Niagara Escarpment from Queenston to Tobermory.

There is a wide array of habitats within Bruce Peninsula National Park. While the forests on the peninsula were largely destroyed by the lumber industry and wildfires in the late 1800s, they have returned as second-growth forests that cover an extensive part of the peninsula. In fact, the upper part of the Bruce Peninsula features the largest remaining area of forest in Southern Ontario. This relatively unfragmented woodland provides vital interior forest habitat for various species that depend on it for survival. Wetlands are also well represented in the park as are a variety of other habitats including rare alvars, old-growth forests, talus slopes, caves, dunes, shorelines and open fields.

Indian Head Cove looks spectacular dressed in white

The second-growth woods in BPNP contain mixed forests consisting of species such as eastern white cedar, trembling aspen and white birch. Coniferous and mixed forests exist along the shorelines and there are also stands of white, red and jack pine. Where deciduous forests occur you are likely to find sugar maple, beech, white birch and red oak.

While these second-growth forests make up much of the upper Bruce Peninsula, an old-growth forest can be found in the area, including in parts of BPNP. An ancient cliff-face forest on the Niagara Escarpment was discovered in 1988 by Doug Larson, a professor at the University of Guelph, and Caedman Nash, a high-school student. Larson and Nash made this incredible discovery while studying the impact of hiking on a cliff-edge forest. What they learned was that the small, gnarled, twisted cedar trees on the cliff face of the Niagara Escarpment grow considerably slower compared to cedar trees growing in forests on level ground – anywhere from 10 to 100 times slower![2] Although small in size, some of the eastern white cedar trees growing on the escarpment cliff faces are hundreds of years old!

Eventually, Larson, members of his Cliff Ecology Research Group at the University of Guelph and Peter E. Kelly determined that some of the living eastern white cedar trees along the Niagara Escarpment were more than a thousand years old.[3]

The magnificent, stunted, cliff-face cedar forest growing on the Niagara Escarpment is not just an old-growth forest but a forest that has changed very little since the last glaciers retreated.

There are various reasons why these ancient cedars are so small for their age and live so long, but the harsh conditions in which they live and the limited space for their root systems have a lot to do with their slow growth rate and longevity. While the cliff-face cedars' roots access cracks and cavities in the rock, they do not have access to quality rooting spaces.

Growing on vertical cliff-faces does have its benefits though. Not only is competition from other plants minimal, but these dangerous

NIAGARA ESCARPMENT

The entire length of the Niagara Escarpment is more than 1,600 kilometres with Ontario boasting approximately 725 kilometres of it. The magnificent rocky ridge, which is over 500 metres above sea level in some locations, began life more than 400 million years ago as the outer rim of a warm, shallow sea.

Today this incredible wilderness corridor provides vital habitat and migration routes for numerous plant and animal species in both urban and rural areas. According to the Niagara Escarpment Commission, the Escarpment is home to more than 300 species of birds, 53 species of mammals, more than 1,500 species of vascular plants, including many rare species, 36 species of reptiles and amphibians along with 90 species of fishes. Some habitats represented here include large, unfragmented forests, vital wetlands, scenic meadows and stunning cliffs. The Escarpment is also where you'll find ancient white cedar forests — with trees as much as 1,000 years old! — clinging to the face of sharp-rising cliffs.

Overseeing the Niagara Escarpment is the Niagara Escarpment Commission (NEC). Formed in 1973, the NEC protects this magnificent eco-corridor. The Niagara Escarpment Parks and Open Space System (NEPOSS) is an important part of the Escarpment connecting more than 160 parks and open spaces via the Bruce Trail.

The Niagara Escarpment was recognized by the United Nations Educational, Scientific, and Cultural Organization (UNESCO) in 1990. When it comes to biosphere reserves, the Niagara Escarpment is in good company with the likes of the Galapagos Islands, the Florida Everglades, Africa's Serengeti and Yellowstone National Park.

For more information:
Niagara Escarpment Commission   www.escarpment.org

How old is this small cedar?

areas are often untouched by humans. Such trees are also too small for timber and agriculture on vertical rock faces isn't practical. When European settlers came to Ontario, they cleared the land for agriculture and timber, leaving the trees and the cliff faces relatively untouched.

Cliffs also protected the trees from fire as is evidenced by the fact that these cliff-face forests survived the fires that ravaged much of the peninsula in the early 1900s.

While studying these fascinating forests Doug Larson and his colleagues also discovered that life was not only flourishing *on* the cliffs, but *in* them as well. Described as *cryptoendolithic*, a term that means "hidden inside rock," the teeming microbial communities discovered inside the rock face are single-celled plants that include green algae and fungi.

Complementing the various types of forests in the park are a variety of wetlands including marshes, fens, swamps, vernal pools, streams, rivers and inland lakes. Wetlands provide important habitat for a variety of species including breeding areas for amphibians. Other animals, including insects, also require water for at least part of their life cycles. Wetlands perform a myriad of other vital functions such as purifying water, controlling flooding, providing oxygen and retaining carbon. Wetlands also provide us with various recreational opportunities including canoeing, kayaking, bird watching and hiking. Unfortunately, Southern Ontario has lost the vast majority of its pre-settlement wetlands to such things as land development, farming

The clear waters of Cyprus Lake

and pollution from agricultural, industrial, commercial and other sources. In fact, 80% or more of Southern Ontario's original wetlands have been destroyed.

The inland lakes in BPNP are typically oligotrophic (low plant growth and low nutrient concentrations), shallow (most have a maximum depth of less than three metres), small and many feature marl (lime-rich) bottoms. Cyprus, Cameron, Emmett, Crane, George as well as Upper and Lower Andrew are some of the larger lakes in, or bordering, the park.

The Cyprus Lake area is popular and has a large campground located on the southeast shore of Cyprus Lake. This lake also connects to Cameron Lake via a narrow passage. A trail goes around the perimeter of Cyprus Lake before meeting up with a few other trails at the northeast end of the lake. These trails go past Horse and Marr lakes before connecting with the Bruce Trail that winds its way along the Georgian Bay coast. This watershed sees Cameron Lake flow into Cyprus Lake which empties into Horse Lake which then flows into Marr Lake before draining into Georgian Bay.

Cyprus Lake is a little under two kilometres long and has a maximum depth of approximately eight metres. Cameron Lake is approximately two and a half kilometres long with a maximum depth of 15 metres. The west side of Cameron Lake lies outside the park. Horse and Marr lakes are considerably smaller

A scenic trail near Cyprus Lake

than Cyprus and Cameron. Both lakes are under half a kilometre long and have maximum depths of around a metre to a metre and a half.

At close to three kilometres long Emmett Lake is another of the larger lakes in the park. It has a maximum depth of approximately 11 metres. George Lake has a depth of about nine metres and is about three and a half kilometres long. Crane as well as Upper Andrew and Lower Andrew lakes are relatively large, shallow bodies of water. Crane Lake is over two kilometres long but only a metre or two at its deepest, while Upper Andrew Lake and Lower Andrew Lake are about one and a half kilometres long with a maximum depth of only a metre or so.

The stunning coastline near Boulder Beach

Marshes, fens, swamps, streams, creeks and rivers are also well represented in BPNP and include Crane River, Willow Creek, William Henry Marsh and Whiskey Still Marsh. Some areas have been given special designations as they represent good examples of a particular natural feature or they are home to threatened or endangered species. For example, the Dorcas Bay Wetland/Meadow is a coastal meadow marsh, and home to a variety of rare species, that is fed by a cold-water stream. This area is a provincial Area of Natural and Scientific Interest (ANSI). Another ANSI is the Niagara Escarpment and the shore in the Rocky Bay area. According to Parks Canada this area is the only remaining undeveloped section of Georgian Bay shoreline in the park. The vicinity also features an ancient cliff forest and is a Dark-Sky Preserve. The Cameron Lake Fen is another ANSI.

A rare habitat present in Bruce Peninsula National Park is the alvar. These limestone barrens are open, flat expanses of calcareous bedrock (dolostone or limestone) with vegetation that includes grasses, sedges along with mosses and lichens often found on the exposed bedrock. Shrubs and trees are also present in areas with more soil. Vernal pools are often present as well. Alvars do not exist in many places around the world. In Southern Ontario they occur on the Canadian Shield, Manitoulin Island and the Bruce Peninsula.

Some other habitats in the park include dunes, talus slopes, caves, Great Lakes shorelines and beaches. The Cameron Lake Dunes is another ANSI. Talus slopes are areas where broken rock accumulates, often at the base of cliffs. The cliffs and the bluffs of the Niagara Escarpment are also home to numerous caves. And the coasts of Lake Huron and Georgian Bay feature a variety of shore and beach habitat.

GEOLOGY

The scenery of the Bruce Peninsula is both breathtaking and varied — from the rugged cliffs of the Niagara Escarpment soaring over Georgian Bay to the gently sloping beaches that ease into Lake Huron. The cliffs and rocky shores in Bruce Peninsula National Park began more than 400 million years ago on the floor of an ancient sea. The large, warm, shallow, tropical sea existed in a depression in the earth that covered what is now Lake Michigan, Lake Huron and Georgian Bay. The centre of the depression was located in what is now Michigan while the whole area is known as the Michigan Basin.

The outer rim of the Michigan Basin is the Niagara Escarpment. This shoreline of the ancient sea extends, in the shape of a horseshoe, from near Rochester, New York south of Lake Ontario, to Hamilton and then north to the tip of the Bruce Peninsula at Tobermory. Between Hamilton and Tobermory

Cyprus Lake Trail in winter

skeletons, which contained calcium carbonate, accumulated on the seafloor where they became compressed into layers of sedimentary rock. The coral reefs, which were also made of calcium carbonate, were also compressed into rock. Sediment such as silt, sand and clay were carried into the sea by rivers. These too became compressed into sedimentary rock. Shale was created from mud, clay and silt while the sand turned into sandstone. Limestone was formed from the skeletons of the invertebrates and the coral reefs. Magnesium, present in the water, was absorbed in the limestone turning it into dolostone (also known as dolomite or dolomitic limestone) which is a harder, more erosion-resistant form of limestone. The caprock of the Niagara Escarpment is dolostone.

the Escarpment passes through places such as Milton, Collingwood and Owen Sound. From Tobermory the Escarpment continues north underwater appearing above water again in the form of islands such as Flowerpot Island, Bear's Rump Island, Manitoulin Island and St. Joseph Island – the most westerly section in Canada. The Escarpment then heads across northern Michigan, down the west side of Lake Michigan and into Wisconsin, ending near the Wisconsin-Illinois border.

Animal life, which included corals, crustaceans and molluscs, abounded in the warm, shallow sea which featured coral reefs. As these marine invertebrates died their

Ontario became a terrestrial environment some 250 million years ago. In his book *Guide to the Geology of the Niagara Escarpment*, Dr. Walter M. Tovell states that at this point the area entered into a long period of erosion.

"By the end of the Paleozoic all marine environments had left southern Ontario. The area became terrestrial and entered a long interval of erosion that ended with the Ice Age. At a minimum this interval must have lasted 245 million years."

Numerous forces have been at work sculpting the sedimentary rocks of the Niagara Escarpment including streams, rivers, ice, wind, waves, rain and glaciers. This shaping process involves rocks of different hardness eroding

The sheltered Marr Lake is a stone's throw from Georgian Bay

at different rates. The harder, more erosion-resistant dolostone caprock overlies the softer shale and sandstone. As these weaker rock layers erode, the caprock becomes unsupported and breaks off creating talus slopes. And while the Escarpment is still susceptible to erosion today and is retreating slowly, it was significantly altered by the glaciers and the post-glacial meltwaters.

Southern Ontario, including the Niagara Escarpment, has experienced at least four periods during the last two million years or so when it was covered in ice sheets two to three kilometres thick. The most recent glaciation, known as the Wisconsin Stage, began up to 100,000 years ago and ended approximately 10,000 years ago. As the glacier advanced it deepened and broadened valleys and left basins carved from the bedrock where some lakes in Bruce Peninsula National Park now exist. The glacier also helped shape the shorelines. As the glacier melted it left behind soil and rock of various sizes that it had carried along as it advanced. There is little glacial till left on the Bruce Peninsula likely as a result of the glacial meltwaters.

Glaciers also deposited large rocks in Bruce Peninsula National Park. Called erratics, these

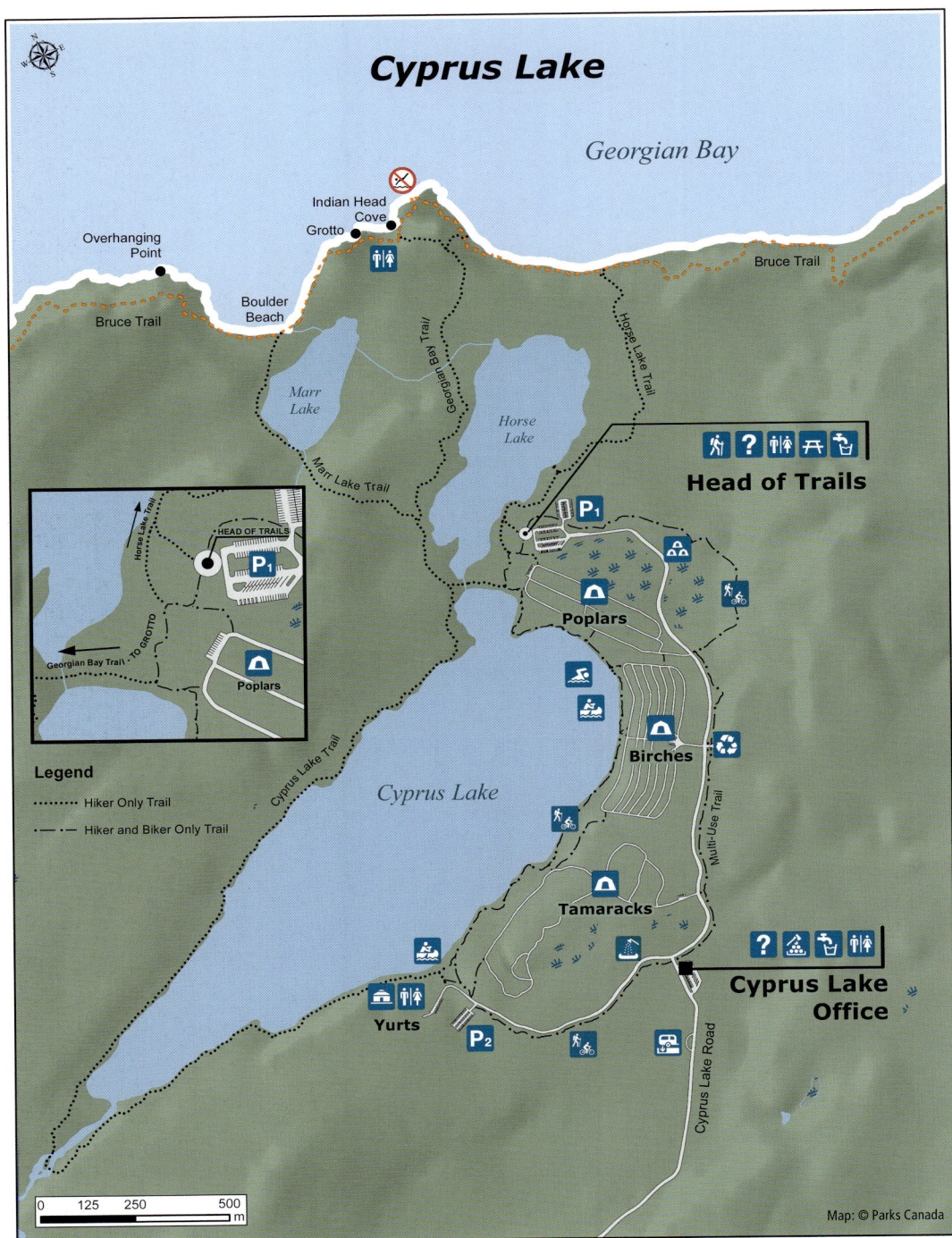

Cedar waxwings at Singing Sands

boulders look different from the surrounding rock because they did not originate here but were instead carried considerable distances by the glacier. Erratics, including some in the Cyprus Lake area and along the rock beaches in the park, were brought here from the Canadian Shield. These erratics are recognized as locally uncommon, speckled-coloured rocks in amongst the predominant greyish-coloured dolostone bedrock.

The glacial ice began melting approximately 14,000 years ago creating a series of post-glacial lakes including the vast Lake Algonquin and the Nipissing Great Lakes. Lake Algonquin existed around 11,000 years ago and covered much of Southern Ontario including the area now occupied by the Lake Huron, Lake Michigan and Georgian Bay basins. At this time much, and possibly all, of the Bruce Peninsula was under water. Several small islands may have been present at the northeast part of the peninsula in the Cabot Head area.

For the next 8,000 years or so the area experienced water levels that changed significantly. The Nipissing Great Lakes, which existed 4,000 to 6,000 years ago, also flooded some of the Bruce Peninsula. The area has also experienced very low water levels where shorelines were well below where they are today. Water levels of Lake Huron have been relatively stable for approximately the last 2,500 years.

The fluctuating water levels of yesteryear and the physical forces of waves from post-glacial lakes have left their marks in many forms in and around BPNP. Overhanging cliffs can be found at numerous points along the Georgian Bay shoreline both inside and outside

Singing Sands is home to numerous plants and birds

the park. The forces of water have also created caves including the Grotto, a popular park attraction located on the Bruce Trail between Boulder Beach and Indian Head Cove. Indian Head Cove also has a sea cave.

The ancient lakes also created sand dunes and beaches. Examples of sand dunes include those located south of Cameron Lake and at Dorcas Bay on Lake Huron. Dorcas Bay also has the popular Singing Sands sand beach. Cobble beaches are also located in the park. Boulder Beach on Georgian Bay at the end of the Marr Lake Trail is a spectacular cobble beach providing views of the scenic shoreline and out to Flowerpot Island and Bear's Rump Island in Fathom Five National Marine Park.

Another fascinating feature carved by the physical forces of water is the sea stack, commonly referred to as a flowerpot, at Little Cove on Georgian Bay in the northwest part of the park.

Beside the sculpting forces of water in and around BPNP, chemical forces have also been doing their part in shaping the rock. BPNP has areas that feature karst topography. A karst landscape is one created by the dissolving action of rainwater on carbonate bedrock such as limestone or dolostone. The natural acidity of rainwater erodes the soluble rock by exploiting crevices and cracks, eventually creating features such as sinkholes, caves, disappearing streams and pit karrens. Pit karrens, or "pitting," are small circular holes in a rock. Karst features occur in many areas including Horse Lake where water drains through a series of sinkholes. You can see good examples of pit karren along the shores of Georgian Bay, Lake Huron and in the Marr Lake area.

FLORA & FAUNA

Bruce Peninsula National Park and its environs have an impressive diversity of plant and animal species including many species at risk. Reasons for the large number of plant and animal species include the high habitat diversity, the relatively low incidence of humans, the region's moderate climate and the large, relatively unfragmented forests. Other factors contributing to the region's diversity include the fact that the Bruce Peninsula is a transition zone between southern and northern vegetation regions, and also a significant migration route for birds.

Approximately 40 mammal species call the northern Bruce Peninsula home, including seven of Ontario's eight bat species. Five of these bat species hibernate in caves along the Niagara Escarpment. Three species of squirrels – red squirrel, northern flying squirrel and eastern grey squirrel – also reside in and around the park.

Two mammals that require large, uninterrupted forests can also be found on

Boardwalk Trail at Singing Sands

the Bruce Peninsula. Fishers were successfully reintroduced to the park area in the late 1970s and early 1980s. Members of the weasel family, fishers are remarkable predators who include porcupines in their diet.

Black bears are also present. Northern Bruce Peninsula is where the southernmost population of black bears reside. This population is genetically distinct from other Ontario bear populations because of their geographic isolation.

The large, mostly unfragmented forests of the northern Bruce also suits the northern flying squirrel and the northern long-eared bat. This area is also the southern limit of the snowshoe hare and the northern limit of the eastern grey squirrel. Other mammals you can catch a glimpse of in the park include white-tailed deer, raccoons, red foxes, coyotes, striped skunks, beavers, muskrats and porcupines. Mink, river otters, various species of mice, and shrews also reside in and around the park.

Bruce Peninsula National Park and its surroundings are blessed with a great diversity of bird species – species that both live and breed in the area as well as species that migrate through it. More than 300 bird species have been recorded living or migrating through the park due in great part to the rich diversity of habitat types such as wetlands, extensive forests, lakes, cliffs and shorelines.

The Peninsula is also located between

There are many trails to explore in Bruce Peninsula National Park

southern-deciduous and northern-boreal forest zones. The report "Bruce Peninsula National Park Management Plan 1998" points out that while many of the birds seen in the area are species common to both the north and south, some species are absent, or rarely seen, in the south.

"The avifauna of the area is decidedly northern in character. A number of boreal species breed in the mixed and conifer woodlands and swamps; most of them are rare or absent farther south. They include olive-sided flycatcher, yellow-bellied flycatcher, ruby-crowned kinglet, common raven, solitary vireo, blackburnian warbler, and northern goshawk. As well, a number of species with southern affinities are in the area, including yellow-billed cuckoo, eastern screech owl, warbling vireo, grasshopper sparrow and wood thrush."

Many forest-interior species of birds are also found in the park and its environs due largely to the unfragmented forests. North America's largest woodpecker, the pileated woodpecker, is one species dependent on such large contiguous tracts of forest.

Birds who prefer wetlands and lakes are also widespread and include the common loon, common merganser, belted kingfisher, great blue heron, herring gull, ring-billed gull and red-winged blackbird while northern harriers and turkey vultures can often be seen soaring above. You might even spot a bald eagle. BPNP is also home to two birds listed under the

Ring-billed gull at Singing Sands

federal *Species at Risk Act* – the least bittern and golden-winged warbler.

While the diversity of bird species is impressive, so too is the diversity of reptiles and amphibians. As many as 30, and possibly more, such species live on the northern Bruce Peninsula. Reasons for the rich diversity include the area's moderate climate, the diversity of habitats including excellent breeding and egg-laying areas, along with a relatively low resident human population.

At least two species of turtles reside in and around the park. There is a possibility that a third turtle population exists. A spotted turtle (which is an at-risk species) was discovered in 2009. Ten species of snakes, including the eastern massasauga rattlesnake, also reside in the park and the surrounding area. Four of these species – eastern milksnake, queen

DARK SKIES OVER NORTHERN BRUCE PENINSULA

We are slowly becoming aware of the importance of dark skies to species — including humans. Artificial lights negatively affect birds who migrate at night; it impacts the foraging and predation patterns of nocturnal animals; and interferes with their orientation and circadian rhythms. Artificial light at night also disrupts our own production of melatonin.

Light pollution has negatively affected the night sky to the point where there are very few places left in Southern Ontario where you can see the stars the way our ancestors saw them. The northern Bruce Peninsula is one place that values dark skies and is one of the last places left in the southern part of the province that truly has dark skies.

Both of the Bruce's national parks — Bruce Peninsula National Park and Fathom Five National Marine Park — received a "Dark-Sky Preserve" designation from the Royal Astronomical Society of Canada in 2009. The Municipality of Northern Bruce Peninsula has been proactive in keeping night skies dark and proclaimed itself a "Dark Sky Community" in 2004.

If you find yourself in the northern part of the Bruce Peninsula on a clear night, look up, look way up and you will see a magnificent world of stars and constellations. And, if you're lucky, the spectacular show might also include the Milky Way, the Northern Lights and stars visible even at the horizon!

For more information on dark skies visit:

Royal Astronomical Society of Canada
http://rasc.ca
International Dark-Sky Association
http://darksky.org

Night sky over Bruce Peninsula Photo: © Robert Dick

snake, eastern massasauga rattlesnake, eastern ribbonsnake – are species at risk.

Amphibians living on the northern part of the Bruce Peninsula include nine species of frogs along with the American toad. Five species of salamander along with the eastern newt and the mudpuppy also make their homes in the park and its environs.

Bruce Peninsula National Park also has a rich diversity of insects with more than 3,000 species recorded, including the monarch butterfly, a species at risk.

The numerous small, shallow lakes in the park are home to a variety of warmwater fish species while some of the larger, deeper lakes have species such as rock bass, pumpkinseed and yellow perch. Crane Lake has a relatively good diversity of fish species including bluntnose minnow, brook stickleback, brown bullhead, Iowa darter and white sucker. Coldwater streams within the park are home to brook trout, brown trout as well as some salmonid species.

There is a good diversity of plants in the park and its surrounding region with the majority of the northern part of the peninsula covered in forest. More than 870 species of vascular plants have been identified within the park. Habitat diversity combined with a moderate climate and a relatively natural environment with minimal human activity has helped create and sustain this rich abundance

Horse Lake

of plants that includes more than 30 species of trees, more than 40 species of orchids, more than 20 species of ferns along with hundreds of species of flowering plants.

Bruce Peninsula National Park is also home to many types of grasses and even 10 species of insectivorous plants, including the pitcher plant. These carnivorous plants live in nutrient-poor soils and get the nutrients they require by trapping and devouring insects.

Dozens of plant species, including many at-risk species, grow on the largely barren alvars. These flat limestone openings are globally rare habitats and home to numerous plant species that are rarely found elsewhere. Lichens, mosses and algae grow well in the extreme alvar conditions. Many of the small, gnarled trees that grow on the alvars on the northern Bruce Peninsula are actually hundreds of years old. Cliffs, talus slopes, wetlands, forests, meadows and beaches are some of the other habitats that contribute to the incredible plant diversity of the northern Bruce Peninsula.

Some of the plant species at-risk in the park include the dwarf lake iris, eastern prairie fringed-orchid, lakeside daisy, Hill's thistle and tuberous Indian-plantain. According to Parks Canada, the northern Bruce Peninsula is home to approximately half the dwarf lake iris that exist in the world and most of the Indian-plantain that exists in Canada.

ACTIVITIES

At more than 150 square kilometres

Winter camping at Cyprus Lake

and with many types of habitat, it is not surprising that there is lots to do at Bruce Peninsula National Park. Activities range from the popular hiking, bird watching and swimming to starwatching, bouldering and winter camping!

A good place to start your experience at BPNP is at the Visitor Centre (which is also the Visitor Centre for Fathom Five National Marine Park) where you can talk to park staff, obtain literature about the park, view the park from a lookout tower and visit the museum.

If you enjoy hiking there are numerous excellent trails in the park that range from easy to difficult. There is close to 25 kilometres of the Bruce Trail in the park. The trail goes from Crane Lake north to High Dump and then follows the stunning Georgian Bay coast to Loon Lake before leaving the park and ending at a cairn in Tobermory's harbour. The cairn marks the northern terminus of the Bruce Trail.

The Singing Sands area of Dorcas Bay features various easy hiking trails including a short boardwalk trail.

Four trails between Cyprus Lake and Georgian Bay offer varying degrees of difficulty. The Georgian Bay Trail is a short, approximately one-kilometre easy hike while the Marr Lake Trail is also fairly short but rated as "difficult." The Horse Lake Trail is just over a kilometre and comes with a difficulty rating of "moderate." If you are interested in a longer, easy walk check out the approximately five-

A yurt on Cyprus Lake

kilometre-long Cyprus Lake Trail.

For campers there is the Cyprus Lake Campground which has more than 230 drive-in campsites in three areas that front onto Cyprus Lake: Birches, Poplars and Tamaracks. There is also a group campsite at the Cyprus Lake Campground along with numerous yurts situated along the shore of this scenic lake. According to Parks Canada these yurts are a "modern version of a traditional dwelling used by the nomads of Central Asia." The semi-permanent, tent-like structures are furnished, have woodstoves and even decks. They are available from spring until fall.

If you are looking for a more remote camping experience there are backcountry

Rocky section of trail

camping areas at Stormhaven and High Dump. These sites are located along the Bruce Trail next to the Georgian Bay shoreline.

Hardy campers can also do some winter tent camping in the Tamaracks area of the Cyprus Lake Campground.

As with hiking and camping there is a good selection of places to go swimming. The extensive sand beach at Singing Sands on Lake Huron is a nice location for families with young children as the water is warm during summer months and quite shallow. Cyprus Lake also provides some swimming opportunities in relatively warm waters.

For those who enjoy a dip in cold water there are opportunities for swimming in Georgian Bay such as at Indian Head Cove. Just be careful of rocks and wavy water conditions — and do not jump from the cliffs – this is dangerous and prohibited.

The many inland lakes are good for those who enjoy canoeing and kayaking. Cyprus Lake is a nice lake to explore and it leads into Cameron Lake via a stream that is usually navigable. Emmett Lake is another of the larger lakes to explore by canoe or kayak.

Birdwatchers will enjoy productive outings in the park. Not only does the park's habitat diversity and its location between southern and northern vegetation regions result in an impressive number of bird species, it's also part of a significant migratory route for birds.

If you enjoy a picnic there are several locations you might try including the Cyprus Lake Campground and the Singing Sands day-use area. Approximately a half-hour or so hike from Cyprus Lake Campground takes you to Indian Head Cove and the Grotto which are top-notch locations for lunch or a snack. Another fine area for an outdoor meal is Halfway Log Dump.

Halfway Log Dump is also a location for bouldering, mentioned earlier. Make sure that you boulder only in the area permitted by the park and that you follow all safety procedures.

Bruce Peninsula National Park is an excellent place to watch the night sky. Light pollution has become such a problem in

Indian Head Cove in fall

Autumn is a quiet time to canoe Cyprus Lake

Southern Ontario that there are few places left where you can enjoy the spectacular show put on by the stars, constellations and Milky Way. Fortunately, this special display is still available by eye on the northern Bruce Peninsula, where the Municipality of Northern Bruce Peninsula, along with Bruce Peninsula National Park and Fathom Five National Marine Park, have been proactive in keeping night skies dark.

If you enjoy winter activities Bruce Peninsula National Park is beautiful covered by snow. Winter activities include winter hiking, cross-country skiing, snowshoeing and winter camping. The trails in winter are not maintained and the shorelines and rocky areas are often icy and hazardous. Be careful where you venture, be prepared for the conditions and take all necessary safety precautions.

For more information: www.parkscanada.gc.ca/bruce

OUR PARK ADVENTURES

While Lynn and I caught a glimpse of Bruce Peninsula National Park when we visited Fathom Five National Marine Park in July, we didn't actually begin exploring the park until early October. It was a beautiful, sunny day when we decided to hike from Cyprus Lake to Georgian Bay and then along the coast on the Bruce Trail. Our original thought was to canoe Cyprus Lake, but strong winds made us rethink this plan and hike the trails instead. It was a wise decision; while Cyprus Lake is a relatively small, shallow lake, the wind had whipped up some significant waves and canoeing in these conditions would be more work than play. The wind and waves, however, had little effect on the mergansers who were racing about the lake.

Our walk began at the southwest part of the lake where we took the Cyprus Lake Trail northeast along the shore, eventually hiking between Cyprus Lake and Horse Lake. We then followed the Georgian Bay Trail next to this small lake and then picked up the Marr Lake Trail that goes along the southwest part of Marr Lake, and then over to Georgian Bay at Boulder Beach where it meets the Bruce Trail. A stellar sight here was the light-coloured waters of Marr Lake in contrast to the dark blue waters of Georgian Bay.

Boulder Beach is a spectacular spot composed of a large rock beach squeezed in between the stunningly beautiful, rugged Georgian Bay shoreline. With the windy conditions we stood here and gazed out at the large waves rolling in and crashing against the shore. In the distance stood Flowerpot Island and Bear's Rump Island. We could have stayed for hours, but we decided to head east along the Bruce Trail to see the Grotto. It is easy to see why this natural cave is so popular, especially during summer months, as its gaping rugged beauty is a thing to behold – especially with

Marr Lake looking east

ORCHIDS OF BRUCE PENINSULA NATIONAL PARK

If you enjoy beautiful flowers in natural surroundings you might consider visiting the Bruce Peninsula in spring where more than 40 species of orchids grow, with more than 30 species having been recorded inside the park itself. Late May to early June is a good time to visit, but orchids and other wildflowers bloom throughout the summer.

Some orchids are hard to find, such as calypso, while others, such as the yellow lady's-slipper can be found growing along roadsides. Some orchids you might come across in the park include Alaska orchid, tall white bog-orchid, spotted coral-root and moccasin flower. You might also want to time your visit so you can attend the annual Bruce Peninsula Orchid Festival that is hosted by the Friends of Bruce District Parks and the Bruce Peninsula National Park.

While enjoying the orchids (and other plants) please make sure you don't harm them. Never try to transplant an orchid. All plants in national parks are protected and removing them is illegal. Orchids are almost never successfully transplanted as they are dependent on their habitat including the fungi with which they have a symbiotic relationship. It is best to enjoy these plants from a distance — so stay on the trails and take a photograph!

For more information on the Bruce Peninsula Orchid Festival visit: www.orchidfest.ca

Yellow lady's slipper

Ram's-head lady's slipper

Butterwort

Lakeside daisy

the large waves from Georgian Bay pulsing in and out of the cave.

Continuing east on the Bruce Trail we soon arrived at Indian Head Cove. While the Grotto may be popular, it is not as impressive as Indian Head Cove in terms of sheer beauty. This inlet with a rock beach surrounded by rock cliffs is truly magnificent. We stayed here for a while taking in the sweeping, soaring landscape. Prior to heading back we hiked a little farther east on the Bruce Trail to a lookout on Georgian Bay that offered more incredible views of the waves smashing against the rocky shoreline.

We took a slightly different route on our return trip. We walked on the Georgian Bay Trail south along the west side of Horse Lake back to where it joins the Cyprus Lake Trail where we once again hiked the east side of Cyprus Lake.

This pleasant, leisurely hike was easily accomplished in two to three hours. Most of the trails were relatively easy for hiking except for the Bruce Trail which I'd rate as moderately difficult to difficult in some areas where you have to carefully navigate the rocky terrain.

****

It was late October when Lynn and I again attempted to canoe Cyprus Lake. It was a cloudless, cool day with a moderate breeze. The conditions were close to ideal for a relaxing paddle around the shallow, tree-

Alvar near Singing Sands

lined lake. On this day, with the exception of a few hikers who were on the Cyprus Lake Trail, we had the entire lake to ourselves.

We had intended to canoe into Cameron Lake which joins Cyprus Lake via some narrows. Unfortunately, some wood debris blocked our route into Cameron Lake so we hauled our canoe up onto some logs to consider the situation. Besides the wood blocking our path, the water level of the lake was low at this time and the water was cold. It quickly became obvious that we would have to carry the canoe for at least a portion of the narrows which, due to the water temperature, was something we were not up for. We made a mental note to canoe Cameron Lake on a future visit.

Cyprus Lake is very clear allowing a good view to the bottom where you'll occasionally sight an old tree. Many of the points are rocky and shallow so we were careful paddling the perimeter of the lake – especially now that the water was cold. While much of the shoreline is comprised of cedars, there are areas where birch and other trees cast their autumn colours of yellow and orange, contrasting with the conifers that grow in abundance. Our relaxed canoe trip around Cyprus Lake, which included frequent stops to observe animals and enjoy the picturesque surroundings, took us a little over an hour.

****

Approximately three months later we found ourselves back at Bruce Peninsula National Park. It was a mild, around 0°C, February morning when we arrived at Cyprus Lake. There wasn't much snow this winter, but it was icy. The trails were in pretty good condition as long as you didn't hurry and you were particularly careful navigating icy sections. The lake itself had ice on it but there was open water around the shore. It was also windy as we walked the Cyprus Lake Trail next to the lake.

When we arrived at the north end of the lake we took the Marr Lake Trail passing the south end of Horse Lake and then proceeded over to the southwest side of Marr Lake. With the protection of the forest we were sheltered from the wind. Next, we headed to Boulder Beach, a cobble beach, which was beautiful – and considerably less windy than when we stood at this spot in October.

After a brief rest on this rocky beach we made our way north and east along the Bruce Trail towards the Grotto and Indian Head Cove. Fortunately, we were wearing high, waterproof boots as considerable water was flowing from Marr Lake into Georgian Bay making the water level in the area significantly higher than on previous visits. Since there hadn't been much snow this winter the trails were accessible – although you had to be extra careful as sections of this part of the Bruce Trail are normally difficult, and potentially dangerous, and being covered in snow and ice they were even more challenging to navigate.

Cyprus Lake where it enters into Cameron Lake

We took numerous photographs of the scenic coast, including the Grotto, before heading over to one of our favourite spots in the park – Indian Head Cove. We carefully made our way down to the shore of the cove and explored the beach and rocks. The view from here, including out to Flowerpot Island and Bear's Rump Island in Fathom Five National Marine Park, was spectacular. Exploring the cove was fascinating and we examined the ancient rocks and marvelled at how the cedar trees thrive living on the rock face with their roots in crevices and cracks.

After resting and relaxing at this cove for a while we took the Georgian Bay Trail that meanders along the west side of Horse Lake and then in between Horse Lake and Cyprus Lake and then returned to the parking lot by taking the Cyprus Lake Trail along the east side of Cyprus Lake. The leisurely hike back from Indian Head Cove took approximately 50 minutes. Near the end of our hike we noticed two tents set up in the Tamaracks Campsite.

Before heading home, tired but exhilarated, we drove down Dorcas Bay Road (a little northwest of Cyprus Lake Road) and checked out where Singing Sands was for a future visit.

****

Lynn and I drove to the park early in the morning to visit Singing Sands in the Dorcas Bay area and take some photographs. It was a warm, sunny day in early June. This area features a beach, wetlands, sand dunes, woods and an alvar along with an impressive diversity of plants.

We began hiking and exploring on the short Boardwalk Trail where we joined a group looking for orchids and other plants. While it wasn't our plan, we had arrived during the Orchid Festival weekend. It was an educational tour where we saw plants such as blue-eyed grass, starflower, Indian paintbrush, wild columbine, fringed polygala along with many others all within a relatively short distance of Singing Sands. Besides orchids such as the ram's head lady's slipper and the yellow lady's slipper, there were also several species of insectivorous plants including the pitcher plant, linear-leaved sundew and butterwort.

After visiting the beach area and hiking trails that took us through a wetland, a forest and an alvar, we drove to another alvar where we went to see the rare lakeside daisy as well as other wildflowers. It was a fine end to another fun day at Bruce Peninsula National Park.

The insectivorous pitcher plant at Singing Sands

One of the "flowerpots" on Flowerpot Island

3. FATHOM FIVE NATIONAL MARINE PARK

"The finest workers in stone are not copper or steel tools, but the gentle touches of air and water working at their leisure with a liberal allowance of time." – Henry David Thoreau

Located adjacent to Bruce Peninsula National Park and at the tip of the Bruce Peninsula separating Lake Huron from Georgian Bay, is Fathom Five National Marine Park. "Fathom Five" became Canada's first National Marine Conservation Area in July 1987 – the same time that Bruce Peninsula National Park was established. Both parks were created by a Federal-Provincial Agreement.

One of the objectives in creating this marine park was to preserve a representative example of the Georgian Bay Marine Region. Fathom Five features one of the few island archipelagos left in the Great Lakes that remains relatively undisturbed. It is also part of the Niagara Escarpment, a biosphere reserve designated by the United Nations Education, Scientific, and Cultural Organization (UNESCO) which recognizes internationally significant ecosystems. Fathom Five is a core protected area of this biosphere reserve. This marine park is also the

> **FATHOM FIVE NATIONAL MARINE PARK**
> - Relatively undisturbed island archipelago
> - Consists of more than 20 islands and islets
> - Home to more than 20 historical shipwrecks and artifacts
> - Features rare habitats such as alvars and ancient cliff-face forests

northernmost park in the Niagara Escarpment Parks and Open Space System (NEPOSS), which includes more than a hundred parks and open spaces from Queenston to Tobermory.

Fathom Five is known for its incredible scenery. It consists of more than 20 islands, and smaller islets, set in the beautiful waters of Lake Huron and Georgian Bay. The park also has a land base near Tobermory where there is a Visitor Centre (which also serves Bruce Peninsula National Park) and hiking trails. Private boaters and shoreline users also make use of the park.

W. Sherwood Fox provides a good description of the waterfront, and the waters, off the northeast tip of the Bruce Peninsula in his book *The Bruce Beckons*.

"Tobermory is two harbours, or rather three. Together the three form two havens, an inner haven for smaller craft and an outer haven for ships of deep draft and heavy burthen. The inner haven consists of two marvellous, canal-like channels that lie close to each other – Big Tub and Little Tub – each cut evenly out of the limestone by an ancient glacier as with an instrument of fine precision. Its perpendicular sides are natural wharves. The outer haven is most impressive – a circular basin three or four

Shipwreck of the *Sweepstakes* in Big Tub Harbour Photo: © Bruce County

miles in diameter shielded from violent winds by an arc of lofty islands that stretches from west to east, a basin spacious enough and deep enough to give safe shelter to a whole navy. Tobermory is one of the great havens of the world."

Two popular recreational activities associated with Fathom Five are boat tours and scuba diving. Companies operate boat tours of the park out from Tobermory that include some of the shipwrecks. They also take passengers to Flowerpot Island.

Fathom Five is also renowned for its scuba diving and snorkelling. The park, and its surrounding waters, feature more than 20 historical shipwrecks and artifacts, as well as submerged geological formations such as cliffs and caves. There are diving opportunities for beginners as well as intermediate and advanced divers. There are also designated snorkel sites.

PARK HISTORY

Before Fathom Five National Marine Park was created in 1987, there was Fathom Five Provincial Park which was established in 1971. Part of the objective in preserving this area as a park was to protect the numerous shipwrecks as well as to support recreational diving in the area. The creation of Fathom Five as a national marine park occurred during negotiations between the federal and provincial governments over Bruce

Flowerpot Island near the sea stacks

Peninsula National Park.

Fathom Five's more than 20 islands include some privately-owned ones as well. The park's land base, just east of Tobermory, covers some 139 hectares. Here you'll find the Visitor Centre, hiking trails and a 20-metre-high tower from which you have a stunning view of Fathom Five as well as the tip of the Bruce Peninsula. The lakebed and water column within the park's boundaries also make up part of this marine park, which is triangular in shape and extends from just west of Tobermory north, encompassing Cove Island east to include Bear's Rump Island and then southwest to Dunk's Bay.

Some of the larger islands in the park include Flowerpot Island, Bear's Rump Island, Cove Island, Echo Island, North Otter Island, South Otter Island, Russel Island and Williscroft Island. Cove Island is the largest in the park at more than 800 hectares. Flowerpot is approximately 200 hectares while Bear's Rump is a little under 100 hectares.

While Fathom Five has been around for some time, first as a provincial park and now as a national marine park, Flowerpot Island has been part of a park for even longer. Flowerpot was acquired from the Province of Ontario by the federal government when it became part of Georgian Bay Islands National Park in 1930. Various islands in the Tobermory archipelago located near Flowerpot Island were also purchased by the federal government and added to Georgian Bay Islands National Park in 1980. Some of the islands that were subsequently transferred to Fathom Five are: Cove Island, Bear's Rump Island, Russel Island, North Otter Island and South Otter Island. Echo Island was purchased in 1996.

Although the history of this park goes back nearly half a century, the area's human history is considerably older. According to a Parks Canada report from 1998, "Fathom Five National Marine Park: Management Plan," Native peoples have lived here for thousands of years.

"The islands of Fathom Five, as well as the surrounding areas of the Bruce Peninsula, were originally home to Native peoples, who hunted, fished, and traded in the region for thousands of years. Archaeological evidence of this use, dating back to 1000 BC, has been found."

During the mid to late 1800s, Europeans came to the upper part of the Bruce Peninsula where, beginning in the 1870s, lumber companies made quick work of the area's vast forests. By 1910 the timber industry was significantly slowing down although smaller lumbering operations continued, including on some of the islands such as Flowerpot, Cove and Bear's Rump. Schooners brought supplies to the lumber towns and left with lumber destined for urban centres in Canada and the United States.

A rock formation on Flowerpot Island

By the mid 1800s, commercial fishing boats plied the waters off Bruce Peninsula with lake trout and whitefish highly sought after. Sailboats were largely replaced by steam tugs in the 1880s which were eventually replaced by gas-powered tugs around the 1930s, a time which also saw a reduction in the number of lake trout caught. While overfishing was largely to blame for the decline in lake trout, so too was the sea lamprey which gained access to the Great Lakes when the Welland Canal opened in 1932. Another threat to lake trout was the

THE WRECK OF THE *BRUCE MINES*

While Fathom Five National Marine Park has an interesting history pertaining to shipwrecks, there are some ships that met their demise in and around the marine park but their exact whereabouts remain unknown. One such ship is the *Bruce Mines*.

Bruce Mines was a steamer built in Montreal in 1842 for the Montreal Mining Company.

After loading up with supplies it left Goderich on November 27, 1854 carrying 26 crew and four passengers. During the night the *Bruce Mines* encountered a terrific gale which battered its hull, causing the ship to leak. In an attempt to keep the steamer afloat the cargo was tossed overboard. Unfortunately, by daylight the next morning the engines were no longer working. In the afternoon land was sighted, although at a considerable distance. It was apparent that the ship would soon go down. Two lifeboats were launched. While attempting to get into one of the boats one of the ship's crew, a carpenter, drowned.

After rowing and bailing for hours in the stormy Lake Huron waters, the two lifeboats landed on two small islands near Cape Hurd. The lifeboats had been launched about three o'clock in the afternoon and landed on the islands around ten o'clock at night.

On November 29 the two lifeboats headed to Owen Sound, the closest inhabited port, where after more than four days the first lifeboat arrived on the night of December 2. The second lifeboat arrived early morning the next day.

It is amazing that only one life was lost in this ordeal. Cargo from the sunken steamer washed ashore where it was salvaged by First Nations people on the Bruce Peninsula.

Although the Bruce Mines is believed to lie in the deep waters off Cape Hurd, the ship's exact whereabouts remain unknown.

Big Tub Lighthouse is a popular tourist location

intentional introduction of rainbow smelt. These factors, all caused by humans, greatly diminished the commercial fishing industry in the area by the 1940s.

The fishing and lumber industries generated significant ship traffic in the area, especially during the last half of the 19th century and the first part of the 20th century. This traffic combined with often perilous weather conditions, including quick rising storms and gales, made for some dangerous trips – particularly in autumn. More than 20 ships were lost within five miles of Tobermory, from September to November, over this period.[4]

Certainly autumn storms had devastating consequences for some ships and their crews, but narrow channels, shoals and islands in the area also took their toll.

Trail on flowerpot Island

The shipwrecks of Fathom Five are scattered throughout the park. They include the *City of Grand Rapids* (steamer) in Big Tub Harbour, the *Cascaden* (schooner) in the southwest section of the park, the *Forest City* (three-masted schooner converted to a steamer) in the northeast part of the park, the *Arabia* (three-masted barque) northeast of Echo Island and an unidentified wreck in Boat Harbour at the northeast part of Cove Island. There are also four shipwrecks – *John Walters* (two-masted schooner), *W. L. Wetmore* (steamer), *James C. King* (three-masted barque converted to a schooner rig and then a barge) and the *Philo Scoville* (three-masted schooner) around Russel Island.

A popular shipwreck is the *Sweepstakes*, a two-masted schooner that now lies at the bottom of Big Tub Harbour. This schooner was built in Burlington, Ontario in 1867. The 36-metre *Sweepstakes* was carrying coal when it was damaged off Cove Island in August 1885 and towed to Big Tub Harbour where it sank in September before repairs could be made. The ship rests in shallow water (maximum depth of approximately seven metres).

Located approximately 30 metres from the *Sweepstakes* lies the *City of Grand Rapids*, a steamer built in Grand Haven, Michigan in 1879. The 37-metre-long passenger steamer

The picturesque Cove Island Lighthouse

caught fire while docked in Little Tub Harbour in October 1907. The burning steamer was towed out of harbour where it drifted into Big Tub Harbour where it sank in shallow water. The *City of Grand Rapids* is another of the more popular shipwrecks in Fathom Five.

In order to make shipping safer, lighthouses were built in and around Fathom Five including the Cove Island Lighthouse, the Flowerpot Island Lighthouse and the Big Tub Lighthouse. The Cove Island Lighthouse was built by stonemason John Brown and was one of many lighthouses that he was commissioned to build. Brown, along with his crew, started the lighthouse and keeper's house, which were made of limestone, in 1855. The 26-metre-high lighthouse was finished in 1856 but it was not operational until 1858. Located on Gig Point on the northeast tip of Cove Island, this lightstation was continually manned from 1858 to 1991 making it the longest light-keeper-occupied station in Ontario. Other structures that were added to the lightstation included a foghorn plant, keeper's houses, a boathouse and a dock.

As you'd expect, this lightstation has a rich history. George Collins was the lightstation's first keeper from 1858 to 1860. The second

A lookout on Burnt Point Loop trail

Red admiral butterfly on pit karrens

keeper, David McBeath, operated it from 1860 to 1872. McBeath and his family ran out of food in their first year here. It was early December 1860 when McBeath, his wife Mary Jane and their five children started to face down starvation – despite having rationed what they had for weeks. McBeath's prior request for supplies had gone unanswered from shore, and with the lake starting to freeze, he had to decide whether he and his family should stay put and hope that provisions would soon arrive, or attempt escape by sail through stormy waters. Fortunately, the treacherous trip was averted; just as the McBeaths were setting sail, a steamer with supplies appeared on the horizon.

Another harrowing tale involves the death of Captain Amos Tripp in 1881. It's described below by Larry and Patricia Wright in their book *Great Lakes Lighthouses Encyclopedia*.

"Like many good lighthouses, Cove Island has its own ghost story. On September 10, 1881, Captain Amos Tripp had just left Goderich with a cargo of salt in his 75-foot (23 m) schooner, *Regina*, when a gale split the oakum calking of its hull, and water flooded the hold. The crew took to the lifeboats, but the captain tried to save the *Regina* on a sand bar off Cove Island. The schooner sank just short of the sand bar, and Captain Tripp's drowned body was later washed ashore. The keeper, George Currie, recovered the body, wrapped it in sailcloth for lack of a coffin, and buried it on the west side of the island. Perhaps the captain was grateful for a decent burial, perhaps not, but after this, there was a supposed 'presence' on the island."

Also located in the park is Big Tub Lighthouse which made traveling the often turbulent waters of Lake Huron and Georgian Bay a little safer. Also known as the Tobermory Lighthouse, Big Tub had a very modest beginning. From 1881 to 1885 Charles Earl hung a lantern from a tree branch at night on the west side of the entrance to Big Tub Harbour. In 1885, John George and David Currie built a hexagonal wooden tower on the site where Earl hung the lantern. The 14-metre lighthouse became automated and electrified in 1952.

Late in the nineteenth century the Flowerpot Island Lightstation was established in what is now Fathom Five National Marine Park. It was built on Castle Bluff on the northeast point of the island in 1897. Perched on a cliff, the lighthouse consisted of a small cottage with a tower for the light beacon. The first lightkeeper was Donald Smith.

In 1901 a new house for the lighthouse keeper was constructed on the shore of the cove west of Castle Bluff. The assistant keeper resided in the house at the light. A fog signal building, which replaced a bell and then a hand horn, was established next to the lighthouse in 1909. Later additions included a dock, a one-storey dwelling built on the beach in 1959, as well as a boathouse/workshop in 1963. In 1969

Big Tub Lighthouse

the original lighthouse was removed and in its place a modern beacon on a steel tower was installed.

HABITATS

Fathom Five National Marine Park, with its numerous islands, mainland base and substantial water base, has a diversity of habitats. The islands in the park are part of the Niagara Escarpment that extends to Manitoulin Island – the largest freshwater island in the world. These islands, due to their isolation and varying distances from the mainland, are unique in terms of the species that live on them. They also provide

The rugged shoreline along the Burnt Point Loop trail

important information about ecosystems.

Some of the larger islands have been logged in the past but now feature mature mixed forests. Other islands, along with the unaltered shorelines on the park's forested mainland base, represent natural areas that have received minimal human disturbance. Beaches, caves, cliffs and talus slopes are also in Fathom Five.

Wetlands are evident on land throughout the marine park and include ponds, fens and marshes. There is also a marl bed on Flowerpot Island and an inland lake, George Lake, on Cove Island.

Alvars are relatively flat, open areas of limestone bedrock. These fascinating habitats exhibit extreme conditions including drought, flooding and extremely hot temperatures. The globally rare habitats have their greatest concentration in North America in the Great Lakes region with some of the most extraordinary alvars occurring on the Bruce Peninsula.

Alvars are also home to numerous plant species, many of which are rare, including wild flowers, lichens and mosses along with algae, grasses and sedges. Bruce Peninsula alvars are also home to such plant species as lakeside daisy, dwarf lake iris and Hill's thistle. Stunted white cedar trees, some of which are hundreds of years old, also grow on alvars.

Some of the animals who can be found in alvars include many species of ground beetles,

Cedars growing on the bluffs of Flowerpot Island

butterflies, leafhoppers, snails and sawflies. Various amphibians, reptiles, mammals and birds also use alvars for part of their life cycles. Species-at-risk birds such as the loggerhead shrike and the bobolink can also be found in alvars making the protection of these rare habitats even more vital.

As with Bruce Peninsula National Park, Fathom Five also features the ancient cliff-face forest of the Niagara Escarpment (for more information on this fascinating forest ecosystem see the "Habitat" section in the chapter on Bruce Peninsula National Park.) In fact, Fathom Five features some of the oldest cedars on the Niagara Escarpment, including a dead tree on Flowerpot Island that was 1,890 years old when it died in 770 CE[5]. There's also a living specimen on Flowerpot that is almost 850 years old named "The Alien."[6]

Fathom Five includes the lakebed and water column within the park. Located where Lake Huron meets Georgian Bay, the park features a variety of aquatic habitats including reefs, marshes, shallow sandy bays, talus rock slopes and deep-water habitats.

Lake Huron is warmer, shallower and murkier compared to Georgian Bay's colder, deeper and clearer waters. Lake Huron is therefore more productive, considering also its shallow inshore habitats. The marine element itself is an oligotrophic ecosystem with clear, well-oxygenated water that is low in nutrients.

There are shoals west of Cove Island with depths of less than eight metres. Much of the park consists of a shelf with depths of 20 to 50 metres at its deepest. The deepest part of the park is located east of Flowerpot Island where it reaches depths of more than 160 metres.

GEOLOGY

Fathom Five is composed largely of water and rock. The rock was formed more than 400 million years ago when a saltwater sea covered a significant portion of North America. When marine invertebrates, including corals, crustaceans and mollusks, died in the warm waters their bodies accumulated on the seafloor. The skeletons of these animals were compressed into layers

The clear waters around Cove Island

Wetlands next to Burnt Point Loop trail

of sedimentary rock which was then carved and shaped by glaciers, wind and water (for a more detailed look at the geology of this area see the "Geology" section in the chapter on Bruce Peninsula National Park.)

Post-glacial lakes played a significant role in many of the marine park's geological features, including sea stacks (flowerpots), sea caves, undercuts and beaches. Ancient lake levels have fluctuated dramatically. Evidence of high-water levels, compared to present-day levels, include sea caves on Flowerpot Island created by waves more than 5,000 years ago. Post-glacial erosion in the form of wave-cut caves and undercuts also appears on Bear's Rump Island.

At other times water levels were much lower than they are today. At one time a land bridge existed between the Bruce Peninsula and Manitoulin Island. The remains of ancient trees over 7,000 years old have been discovered still rooted to the lakebed in Fathom Five!

A popular feature of Fathom Five are the wave-cut sea stacks located on Flowerpot Island's eastern shore. These "flowerpots" were once part of the main escarpment. They were formed when waves eroded the less resistant rock of the cliff. As lake levels continued to drop, ongoing erosion left the more resistant rock pillars. Parks Canada has cemented parts of the sea stacks to slow the erosion process. The two flowerpots are approximately 12

Juvenile merlins

a considerable waterfall which later became an "enormous set of rapids some 800 metres (2,640 feet) long, 1,000 metres (3,300 feet) wide and with a drop of 40 metres (132 feet). It likely carried as much or more water than Niagara Falls does today." This "waterfall" now lays submerged in Georgian Bay.

FLORA & FAUNA

Since Fathom Five National Marine Park has a 139-hectare land base next to Bruce Peninsula National Park, many plants and animals will be found in both parks (see "Flora & Fauna" in the chapter on Bruce Peninsula National Park for additional information.)

metres and 7 metres high.

Another wild geological feature in Fathom Five is the "pop-up" situated northeast of Echo Island. According to Parks Canada, this pop-up, also known as a "rock heave" or "pressure ridge," is one of the largest in Southern Ontario with a length of 1,750 metres and a height of up to five metres.

A particularly fascinating landform discovered in the park is a "submerged waterfall". At a time when water levels were low, much of what is now Fathom Five was dry land except for rivers and waterfalls. These drained from what is now Lake Huron into Georgian Bay and across to and then down the Ottawa River. According to Parks Canada, one of the rivers near Middle Island formed

However, another interesting component of Fathom Five's plant and animal species pertains to the park's island biogeography. Each of the islands, due to their size, isolation, and distance to the mainland has its own unique flora and fauna. Cove Island is the park's largest island and is also close to the mainland and other islands. It therefore has a relatively good diversity of wildlife species that includes whitetail deer, black bear and the massasauga rattlesnake.

Red squirrels live on Flowerpot Island, but the eastern chipmunk does not. Both species live on the mainland, but since the eastern chipmunk hibernates and is not awake when Georgian Bay freezes over, thus creating an ice bridge to the islands, this animal has not

Green frog on pit karrens

been observed on any of the islands. This ice bridge does not reach all islands every year, and some of the more remote islands will only occasionally be joined to the mainland by ice. Other animals who hibernate, such as the groundhog, will also likely not be observed on the islands of Fathom Five.

Animals who are active during the winter are often found on numerous islands in the area and include the snowshoe hare, the red fox, the deer mouse and the coyote.

Fathom Five is an established migratory corridor for birds and more than 250 species have been recorded here including raptors, colonial waterbirds, shorebirds and songbirds.

Some of the colonial waterbirds who reside in Fathom Five include the great blue heron, the double-crested cormorant, the black-crowned night heron, the common tern, the herring gull and the ring-billed gull. Songbirds are also well represented in the park and make up the majority of bird species in Fathom Five. The bald eagle and the whip-poor-will are two species at risk in Fathom Five.

Numerous species of amphibians and reptiles can be found on the park's islands and mainland property. Amphibians such as the yellow-spotted salamander, the redback salamander, the American toad, spring peeper and the green frog have all been recorded on at

Flowerpot Island

least several of Fathom Five's islands. Reptiles such as the northern watersnake, the eastern gartersnake, the northern ringneck snake and the Midland painted turtle also reside on several islands in the park. The massasauga rattlesnake also lives on at least one park island.

Fathom Five also features numerous species of insects. The area is a transition zone that includes species from both northern and southern faunas. The monarch butterfly is one at-risk species found in the park.

The waters of Fathom Five also include a large diversity of life. Plankton includes phytoplankton (plants) and zooplankton (animals) living and drifting in the water and providing an important source of food for other zooplankton, invertebrates and fish. Various organisms, including benthic invertebrates, live in the lakebed providing a food source for fish. This community has experienced the introduction of non-native species such as zebra and quagga mussels.

More than 100 fish species have been recorded in Lake Huron and many of these would be present in the waters of Fathom Five. The fish community in and around Fathom Five has changed considerably during the last century and a half and these changes can be attributed to humans.

Commercial fishing has been in the area

since the 1830s and by the mid-nineteenth century there were plenty of commercial boats working off the Bruce Peninsula. Lake trout was the fish of choice. Lake trout populations were in decline as early as the late 1800s due to overfishing and by the 1940s local lake trout populations had been decimated. Another significant impact to the lake trout involved sea lamprey predation. Sea lampreys gained access to Lake Huron via the Welland Canal in the 1930s.

The introduction of other non-native fish species into Lake Huron has also affected native fish communities. Some of the non-native fish species that have impacted the Lake Huron ecosystem include rainbow trout, carp, rainbow smelt, alewife, coho and chinook salmon. Many non-native fish species in Lake Huron were intentionally introduced.

Non-native invertebrates in Lake Huron have also been destructive to the ecosystem. The spiny water flea, a species of zooplankton native to Europe and Asia, was first noticed in Lake Huron in 1984. Zebra mussels, freshwater molluscs native to Europe and Asia, were found in all of the Great Lakes by 1990. Both of these non-native species were introduced to the Great Lakes in ballast water discharged from transoceanic ships. Some of the at-risk fish species in Fathom Five include the lake sturgeon, the shortjaw cisco and the deep-water sculpin.

Burnt Point Loop is part of the Bruce Trail

Due to the many types of habitats in Fathom Five there are numerous species of plants. The islands of this marine park contain more than 500 such species from the ancient cedars to mixed forests to lichens, mosses and grasses found on alvars. The Bruce Peninsula, including Fathom Five, is home to a rich diversity of ferns including the rare northern holly fern and the wall rue.

While the Bruce Peninsula is known for its diversity of flora, it may be best known for the more than 40 species of orchids that grow here, many of which are in Fathom Five including the calypso orchid and the Alaska orchid.

ACTIVITIES

Fathom Five is a marine conservation area with a rich history and many of the activities within the park are associated with its past. The park's scenic islands and more than 20

THE FRIENDS OF THE BRUCE DISTRICT PARKS ASSOCIATION & THE FLOWERPOT ISLAND LIGHTSTATION

The Friends of the Bruce District Parks Association promotes awareness and education of natural, historic and cultural resources in Bruce Peninsula National Park and Fathom Five National Marine Park. This association has helped restore the Flowerpot Island Lightstation.

In 1998 the group began its Volunteer Lightkeeper Program which allows individuals or families the opportunity to be lightkeepers at this historic lightstation. Lightkeepers have duties to perform during their stay including greeting visitors, selling snacks and souvenirs and maintaining the lawn and gardens. Accommodations are located in the one-story dwelling built in 1959.

If this "working vacation" interests you contact The Friends of the Bruce District Parks Association, www.castlebluff.com, email: infoatcastlebluff@gmail.com

Flowerpot Island Lightstation

This sea stack, also known as a "flowerpot", on Flowerpot Island was once part of the main escarpment

Burnt Point Loop trail

historical shipwrecks, combined with several lighthouses and trails on the mainland property and Flowerpot Island, ensure that there is plenty to see and do.

The land base features a Visitor Centre, which it shares with Bruce Peninsula National Park, along with a 20-metre-high tower that provides beautiful views over the marine park and the tip of the Bruce Peninsula. Here you can enjoy a hike on the Burnt Point Loop trail, a side trail of the Bruce Trail. This approximately four-kilometre-long footpath offers beautiful views, from several lookouts, out over the water and islands of Fathom Five, as well as Georgian Bay's stunning coast, including Little Dunk's Bay.

Private tour-boat companies in Tobermory operate cruises through Fathom Five along with trips to Flowerpot Island. These tours provide spectacular views of the marine park including some of its islands, shipwrecks and lighthouses. Some of the tours are nonstop while others allow passengers a visit to Flowerpot.

This fascinating island is located a little more than six kilometres from Tobermory.

Visitors will find lots to do including a trip to see the two flowerpots (sea stacks) up close. A short hike from the flowerpots takes you to a cave created by waves more than 5,000 years ago. This was the shoreline of what used to be Lake Nipissing. Trails also allow you to visit Beachy Cove and the lightstation which is maintained by The Friends of the Bruce District Parks Association. This association, through its Volunteer Lightkeeper Program, offers members the opportunity to be modern-day lightkeepers. Other activities on Flowerpot include picnicking, swimming and camping. In fact, Flowerpot is the only island in Fathom Five where you can camp. The small number of tenting sites are located near Beachy Cove.

Boating is another way to enjoy Fathom Five. While there are no docks or facilities at the park's islands (except for Flowerpot Island), you can visit these places to explore and maybe have a picnic, but camping and fires are prohibited. Due to the possibility of rough waters and the fact that weather conditions can change very quickly here, Parks Canada recommends that only experienced paddlers canoe or kayak on Georgian Bay and Lake Huron.

SCUBA diving and snorkelling are popular activities due largely to the park's numerous well-preserved shipwrecks and fascinating underwater geologic features. There are numerous snorkel sites in Fathom Five as well as diving sites for beginners, intermediate and advanced divers.

For more information: www.parkscanada.gc.ca/fathomfive

OUR PARK ADVENTURES

The first trip that Lynn and I made to the tip of the Bruce Peninsula was in late July. The lush forests not only looked inviting but smelled wonderful. We got a great view of the Bruce's unfragmented forests and the incredible blue waters of Fathom Five from a 20-metre tower located near the Visitor Centre.

You don't have to have a boat to enjoy this marine park as there are inviting trails on the park's mainland property that take you to scenic lookouts along the shores of Georgian Bay where the bay's islands and pristine turquoise waters were on display. Our hike brought us to two young merlins perched in the top of a tree as well as kayakers exploring the clear waters of the rugged coastline.

****

It was a warm, hazy day in early September when Lynn and I were treated by Parks Canada to an exciting tour of the waters and islands of Fathom Five National Marine Park. We began our journey in Big Tub Harbour and headed northwest passing Russel Island. This island features rocky shores with cedar and other conifers. There are also four shipwrecks just off this island.

Continuing on in a northwest direction we

Kayakers exploring Georgian Bay shoreline in the marine park

Glacial erratic

passed between Turning and Williscroft islands as we headed for Cove Island. Cove is a large island that has an inland lake – George Lake. Cove Island boasts a rugged shoreline with lots of inlets, wetlands and isles. The blended colours of rock, water, lichen, trees and other plants were beautiful.

We travelled along the western shore of Cove Island before heading northeast to Gig Point at the northeast tip. Cove Island Lighthouse is located here. Built in 1858, the 24-metre structure is an eye-catching piece of architecture and history.

After rounding Gig Point, we headed in a southeast direction going past Echo Island on our way to the famous Flowerpot Island. Approaching the northeast side we were treated to the magnificent bluffs with cedar trees clinging to the rock formations. This island also has a lighthouse and through The Friends of the Bruce District Parks Association you can apply to be a short-term lightkeeper. Duties include meeting visitors.

The flowerpots are on the east side of the island. These incredible rock formations are definitely the focal point of a rocky shoreline featuring flat rock areas with steep bluffs, turquoise water and views of Bear's Rump Island in the distance. We went ashore next to one of the flowerpots and hiked a short distance up to a sea cave.

We then checked out Little Cove as well as a boat wreck in Little Tub Harbour before heading back.

What an enjoyable trip!

Viewing tower

Island 176

4. GEORGIAN BAY ISLANDS NATIONAL PARK

"Water is the driving force of all nature." – Leonardo da Vinci

Stretching approximately 50 kilometres along the eastern shore of Georgian Bay, from Beausoleil Island in the south to Twelve Mile Bay in the north, is Georgian Bay Islands National Park (GBINP). This incredibly beautiful park features the rugged Canadian Shield landscape including the windswept pines that Group of Seven painters helped make famous.

The water-access only park includes islands, or parts of islands, and shoals along with a small land base in Honey Harbour. In total, GBINP administers 48 islands along with a series of lots in southeast Georgian Bay. Beausoleil Island is the largest in the park. It was designated a Canadian national historic site in 2009.

Created in 1929, Georgian Bay Islands National Park was the third national park to be established in Ontario (and the third in eastern Canada). At approximately 14 square kilometres, this park is Canada's smallest national park.

GEORGIAN BAY ISLANDS NATIONAL PARK
- Highest diversity of reptiles and amphibians of any of Canada's national parks
- Remote rocky islands and windswept stands of white pine
- Presence of the eastern massasauga rattlesnake
- Part of the planet's largest freshwater archipelago

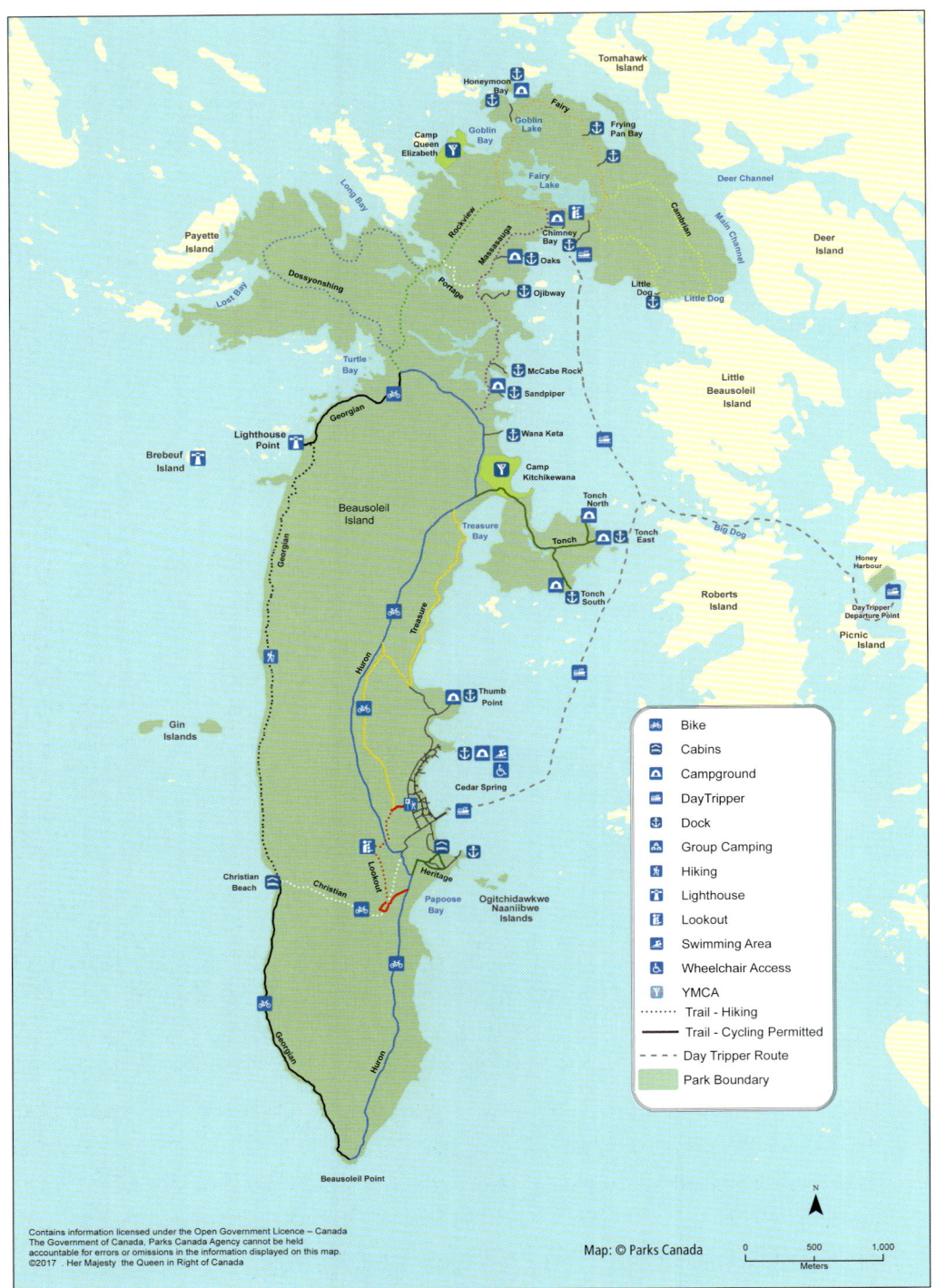

Georgian Bay Islands National Park is part of the Georgian Bay Biosphere Reserve which was organized by the United Nations Educational, Scientific, and Cultural Organization (UNESCO) in 2004. Both the park and the biosphere reserve are part of the Thirty Thousand Islands – the planet's largest freshwater archipelago!

While GBINP is our smallest park, it comes with a fascinating human history going back thousands of years. The park is also home to 33 species of reptiles and amphibians. This rich diversity of herpetofauna is higher than what is found in any of Canada's other national parks. Plants are also well represented here with approximately 800 species recorded here. Georgian Bay Islands National Park straddles two natural regions.

Boardwalk at Cedar Spring on Beausoleil Island

Parks Canada sign on Island 176

The island-based park offers a variety of activities including boating and sailing as well as hiking, swimming, picnicking and nature appreciation. You can explore any of the islands by day, but only Beausoleil Island permits camping. Activities on Beausoleil include: camping, hiking, cycling, swimming, picnicking, photography, canoeing, kayaking, and birdwatching. If you do not have a boat, you can access Beausoleil Island on the park's *DayTripper* which departs from Honey Harbour.

PARK HISTORY

Georgian Bay Islands National Park was created in December of 1929. The park consisted of Beausoleil Island along with 28 smaller islands. At this time Beausoleil was the last remaining large island in Georgian Bay that was not privately owned. It is eight kilometres long by about a kilometre and a half wide.

While the park was officially established in 1929, the proposal to create such a park in Georgian Bay came about almost a decade earlier when Dr. C. B. Orr, with the Provincial Museum of Toronto, recommended the idea to the Commissioner of National Parks.[7]

Just as Orr had advocated for Beausoleil Island in his 1920 proposal, the next year Harry Tucker of Owen Sound argued that Flowerpot

GEORGIAN BAY BIOSPHERE RESERVE

Georgian Bay Islands National Park is part of the Georgian Bay Biosphere Reserve. This reserve was designated by the United Nations Educational, Scientific, and Cultural Organization (UNESCO) in 2004. Extending 200 kilometres along the eastern coast of Georgian Bay, from Port Severn to the French River, it encompasses 347,000 hectares and includes core protected areas, buffer areas and a transition area. The core protected areas include GBINP along with five provincial parks while the surrounding buffer areas consist largely of Crown lands and First Nations' lands. The transition area includes communities practising sustainable development. GBINP plays a significant role within the biosphere reserve by promoting ecotourism, education, environmental stewardship and protection.

The Georgian Bay Biosphere Reserve encompasses the Thirty Thousand Islands and includes numerous habitats amongst the scenic bays, shores, beaches, shoals, islands, forests and wetlands. The biosphere reserve features a rich biodiversity that consists of many species at risk including numerous species of turtles and snakes as well as the five-lined skink. Two butterflies – the monarch butterfly and the West Virginia white butterfly – are also at-risk species.

Mammals on the at-risk list include some bat species and the Algonquin wolf while the butternut tree, forked three-awned grass and the broad beech fern are three plant species also on the list. There are three at-risk species of fish in the area – lake sturgeon, northern brook lamprey and silver lamprey – while the western chorus frog is the only at-risk amphibian. There are close to 20 species of birds that are at-risk in the Georgian Bay Biosphere Reserve including: bald eagle, bobolink, whip-poor-will, rusty blackbird, least bittern, barn swallow, common nighthawk, Canada warbler and the cerulean warbler.

The non-profit Georgian Bay Biosphere Reserve Inc. was established in 1998. Their mission includes working with other groups and organizations supporting the conservation of biodiversity and sustainable development.

For more information on the Georgian Bay Biosphere Reserve visit: www.gbbr.ca

Fairy Lake, Beausoleil Island

Island also deserved to be part of a national park. Tucker's recommendation became a reality in 1930 when Flowerpot was purchased for $165 and made part of Georgian Bay Islands National Park. Flowerpot Island became part of Fathom Five National Marine Park when FFNMP was created in 1987. Over the years more islands have been added to the park.

Beausoleil Island itself also has a fascinating history. As a national park it goes back less than a century, but as a home for Aboriginal Peoples its story goes back thousands of years. Artifacts have been found here that date as far back as 7,000 years. Tools, pottery and hunting items have all been found on Beausoleil Island.

By the early 17th century Beausoleil was visited by Native Peoples and Europeans, including fur traders and missionaries. Back then the island was known by various names. The Huron called it Skiondechiara, which means "The Land to Appear Floating Afar," while the French knew it as Isle du Traverse. In Ojibwa, the island was called Pamendenagog which means "Island That Floats in the Water" while the British named it Prince William Henry Island. But the name we know today stems from a French-Canadian named Beausoleil who settled on the southern tip of the island in 1819. People soon began referring to the large island as Beausoleil's Island — and

Cemetery of the Oak, Beausoleil Island

it stuck, minus the apostrophe "s."

Increasing European settlement in the area impacted every element of Native life and it wasn't long before local Native people experienced forced relocation to reserves. By 1842, Beausoleil Island was an Ojibwa Reserve under the leadership of Chief John Assance. The Beausoleil Band pursued an agricultural lifestyle living in what is now the island's Cedar Spring area. More than 80 hectares of land was cleared to grow corn and potatoes. These fields are still evident today in the form of a meadow. The settlement consisted of more than 230 people and included numerous log houses, barns and a church. A nearby cemetery, Cemetery of the Oak, is located where the main settlement was.

Unfortunately, the land was not very fertile and crop failures were common. Besides corn and potatoes, fish and maple sugar were also obtained, but life was very difficult and not sustainable. In 1856, Treaty 76 surrendered Beausoleil Island, along with other islands in Georgian Bay, to the government.

Most residents moved to Christian Island, located a little west of Beausoleil, around 1858. Here more fertile soil awaited. When Georgian Bay Islands National Park was established in 1929, only three families were living on Beausoleil Island – the Tonchs, the Tobeys and the Corbières, which explains park names such as Tonch Point and Tobey Dock.[8]

HABITATS

Georgian Bay Islands National Park has an impressive diversity of habitats. Some habitats featured in this incredible archipelago include rocky outcrops and other open areas, various wetlands and forests.

Rocky outcrops are synonymous with the Thirty Thousand Islands area. These exposed rocky areas feature few animal and plant species compared to other habitats. Some of the first plants to grow in these harsh, exposed environments were lichens which are a combination of algae and fungi. These plants help create soil which allows other plants, such as grasses and mosses, to grow in these shallow soils and in harsh conditions. Bushes and some trees such as white pine and red juniper also take hold in these marginal areas with minimal soil and strong north-westerly winds. Various birds such as prairie warbler, yellow warbler, hairy woodpecker and white-breasted nuthatch, live in the vegetation amongst, and surrounding, these rock outcrops as do animals such as chipmunks and mice as well as snakes who can often be found sunning themselves on the rocks.

Georgian Bay Islands National Park and its environs are home to a variety of wetlands including marshes, swamps, bogs, ponds and

Camping on Beausoleil Island

Boardwalk across wetlands on Beausoleil Island

vernal pools. These wetlands are important habitat and one reason why the area has such a rich biodiversity.

Marshes are commonly found on the eastern shores of islands and these productive wetlands that are rich in nutrients are home to numerous plants, birds, amphibians, reptiles, mammals, insects and fishes. Various species of turtles and frogs are some of the herpetofauna found in the park's marshes as well as fish such as yellow perch, pumpkinseed and carp.

Bogs and ponds are also found in the Georgian Bay area. Glaciers are responsible for creating bogs as these massive sheets of ice gouged out depressions and hollows in the land. Bogs are often deep, stagnant ponds where the water has a high acidity. Sphagnum moss is common here.

Beaver dams are also responsible for creating bogs and ponds. Turtles, frogs and snakes, including the eastern massasauga rattlesnake, are found in these habitats as are a variety of insects, birds and mammals.

Swamps are another habitat found in GBINP which are really wet forests. These nutrient-rich wetlands, which can be flooded seasonally or for long periods, are often created on islands due to poor drainage. They feature tree species that are water tolerant such as white cedar, yellow birch and willow. Ferns also do well in these wet environments.

Vernal pools are another wetland found on the islands. Vernal pools contain water for part of the year and often dry out in late summer. The water comes from rain and snowmelt. Since they occasionally dry out vernal ponds do not contain fish populations, making them good habitat for breeding frogs, toads, salamanders and other amphibians. A variety of insects and other animals also depend on vernal pools for at least part of their life cycle.

Mixed forests are another habitat found in the park. Some forests, such as those in the southern part of Beausoleil Island, feature thick till layers left here by the glaciers. These lush forests are home to maple, beech and oak. The southern part of Beausoleil Island is extensively covered in mature, hardwood forest. But not far away, including the northern part of the park and even the northern section of Beausoleil Island, are the boreal forests of the north which contain considerably less soil.

Georgian Bay Islands National Park lies on the edge of the Canadian Shield and is part of a transition area that is home to many northern and southern species of plants and animals.

GEOLOGY

Georgian Bay Islands National Park is located on the south-western edge of the Canadian Shield which features rocks that are over a billion years old. The prominent rock featured in the Thirty Thousand Islands area is gneiss which geologist and writer

Vernal pool on Gray Island

Beautiful rock formations on Island 221

Nick Eyles describes in *Road Rocks Ontario: Over 250 Geological Wonders to Discover*: "strikingly beautiful outcrops of complexly folded billion-year-old gneiss dominate these remote rocky islands and their windswept stands of white pine."

Eyles also describes the beginnings of the Canadian Shield that occurred long ago.

"The first stage in the development of the Canadian Shield took place about 1,000 million years ago when the majestic Grenville Mountains, that had been thrust up during the Grenville Orogeny, were eroded and flattened to a level plain. These mountains might have been the tallest in Earth history."

Fast forward to *only* a little more than 400 million years ago when the area was covered by a warm, shallow sea. Sediments accumulated on the seafloor and these were compressed into rocks such as sandstone, limestone and shale lying on top of the harder, ancient rock surface of gneiss and granite-gneiss. Erosion in the south-eastern area of Georgian Bay, including Georgian Bay Island National Park, has removed the younger, sedimentary rocks leaving behind islands of ancient rocks.

When glaciers appeared between two million and 14,000 years ago, these massive ice sheets further rounded and smoothed the rock of Georgian Bay's eastern shore while removing much of the soil. These glaciers also left large boulders – erratics – that can be seen in the now forested areas of Beausoleil Island.

The northern end of Beausoleil Island is another area of GBINP where the work of a glacier has left its mark. Fairy Lake, located at the north end of Beausoleil Island between Chimney Bay and Goblin Lake, was created when a glacier gouged out a basin which was then dammed by glacial debris.

When the most recent glacier began to melt and retreat approximately 14,000 years ago it created a series of post-glacial lakes, including Lake Algonquin which existed around 11,000 years ago. At one time Lake Algonquin covered Beausoleil Island, at other times lake levels were significantly lower than they are today. While water levels have changed considerably, Lake Huron has had relatively stable water levels for approximately the last 2,500 years.

Glaciation is also responsible for much of what you find on the shores of GBINP. The beaches are composed of glacial sand left behind after they scraped the land and melted. The southern part of Beausoleil Island also contains sand and gravel deposits left by the last glacier.

The islands of GBINP continue to change – albeit slightly from a geological perspective. Weathering and erosion crack the rock and

Ojibway Bay, Beausoleil Island

Midland painted turtle

waves loosen and remove the rock as well. This process in the Thirty Thousand Islands area is extremely slow due to the hardness of the ancient rocks and the changing water levels which results in waves attacking different sections of the shore at different times. Those who don't like change can take comfort in knowing that the island rock here has changed little in the approximately 10,000 years since the last glacier retreated.

FLORA & FAUNA

At first glance you might think that a park consisting of mostly small, rocky islands would not have a rich biodiversity. But you would be wrong in the case of this park's flora and fauna. This small park, consisting of islands stretching 50 kilometres along the east shore of Georgian Bay, features approximately 800 species of plants. Thirty-three species of reptiles and amphibians, the most found in any of Canada's national parks, also reside here.

The park's biodiversity increases as you travel from the outer islands toward the inner islands. The outer islands are exposed to harsh conditions; hold little soil; are isolated from the mainland; and are constantly exposed to strong winds and large waves. These conditions result in considerably fewer species compared to the less exposed middle islands, inner islands and the mainland. Plants found on some of the outer islands include lichens, grasses, sedges, bushes and some dwarfed trees such as white pine.

The beautifully stark, desolate outer islands are frequented by some birds such as song sparrows, yellow warblers and spotted sandpipers. Colonies of gulls and terns also inhabit outer islands. Herring gulls live in large colonies on some of the outer islands such as Gray Island. Ducks and loons can also be found among the outer islands as well as shorebirds and other birds who use these isolated landforms to rest while migrating. Besides birds there aren't many other animals, with the exception of northern watersnakes who swim their way to the outer islands. In the cold waters surrounding the outer islands are fish such as lake whitefish, walleye and white bass.

Besides providing homes and shelter to some species, the outer islands offer protection to the middle islands which in turn provide protection to the inner islands and the mainland. There is richer biodiversity on the middle and inner islands.

Much of the park's biodiversity is found on Beausoleil Island. At close to 11 square kilometres, it is by far the largest island in the park. It also features both hardwood forests, which grow in the thicker soils on the southern part of the island, and boreal forests, found on the island's rocky, windswept northern section.

GBINP is in a transition zone on the edge of the Canadian Shield which is home to both northern and southern species of plants and

Insects enjoying milkweed on Beausoleil Island

EASTERN MASSASAUGA RATTLESNAKE

The east side of Georgian Bay, including Georgian Bay Islands National Park, is one of only four areas in Ontario where the eastern massasauga rattlesnake is known to live. Massasaugas also live on the Bruce Peninsula, including Bruce Peninsula National Park, as well as small populations in the Windsor and Wainfleet (near Port Colborne) areas.

Ontario's only venomous reptile, massasaugas have a thick, grey or tan coloured body with a row of large, dark blotches down the centre of the back and several rows of smaller, alternating dark blotches on the sides. The dorsal pattern is unique for each snake and can be used for identification purposes. Most massasaugas are 45 to 75 centimetres long, have a triangular head and a rattle at the end of their tail which they use as a warning signal. When the massasauga is born there is a single segment, called a "button," at the end of the tail. Whenever the snake sheds, a new segment is added to the rattle. Segments later break off as the rattle continues to grow.

The eastern massasauga rattlesnake's head is relatively wide and features a white stripe and three black stripes. These stripes begin at the snake's face and extend back towards the animal's neck.

The word massasauga is from the Chippewa word for "great river-mouth" which alludes to the marshes at the mouth of the rivers where the snake was often found. Anywhere from 6 to 20 young are born in late July or August and these snakes are on their own from the beginning. Those fortunate to survive their juvenile stage may live as long as 18 years. Snakes must hibernate to survive and this occurs in a hibernaculum that is below the frost line and above the water table. A snake hibernaculum is an underground chamber where a snake is protected from the cold and can include animal burrows, rock

Massasauga's have relatively wide heads

Eastern hog-nosed snake. This species is often incorrectly identified as an eastern massasauga rattlesnake.

crevices and tree root cavities.

Massasaugas live in a variety of habitats including forests with an open canopy (they need open areas where they can warm up in the sun), rocky areas, marshes and swamps, bogs and fens as well as tall-grass prairie. Diet is made up largely of small mammals such as mice, shrews and voles as well as other animals including frogs.

Massasaugas are shy, timid animals who try to avoid humans whenever possible. Bites often occur when the snake is accidentally stepped on or a person attempts to handle the snake. Records indicate that only two people in Ontario are known to have died from massasauga bites and in both cases the victims did not receive the proper treatment.

There are many things you can do to reduce the chances of being bitten when you are in massasauga country. Learn to identify this snake and be able to distinguish it from similar-looking snakes such as the eastern foxsnake, the eastern hog-nosed snake, the northern watersnake and the eastern milksnake. Wear long pants and footwear that offers protection, such as boots. Never bother or threaten a snake and do not attempt to pick one up. Be aware of where you walk and put your hands. If you hear a rattle stay calm and determine its location, then slowly move away from the snake. If you are traveling at night use a flashlight. Always keep animal companions on leashes. And teach your children and educate others about these safety tips.

It is important to learn first aid procedures which will come in handy if you are with someone who has been bitten. It is important to remain calm and to keep the person who was bitten calm. Arrange for the victim to be transported to the hospital as a person who has been bitten by a massasauga requires medical treatment. Wash and clean the wound and remove any jewellery from the bitten limb in case swelling occurs. Loosely splint the affected limb and, if possible, keep it below heart level. If the victim is waiting for transportation lay them down and keep them calm and inactive to help slow the circulation of venom through the body. Try to identify or be able to describe the snake. If possible, photograph the snake for identification purposes if you have a cell phone or camera with you.

If your animal companion has been bitten, try to keep her calm and inactive. Signs of bites include swelling, pain or discomfort. Splint the affected limb if possible and try to keep it below heart level. If possible, carry your animal companion and take her to a veterinarian immediately.

The eastern massasauga rattlesnake is an at-risk species listed as nationally threatened by the Committee on the Status of Endangered Wildlife in Canada. Massasaugas are protected by both federal and provincial legislation and penalties for killing, harming, harassing or capturing a massasauga are significant.

Although the massasauga is an at-risk species facing many threats, there are people attempting to protect this important, docile reptile including the Eastern Massasauga Rattlesnake Recovery Team that includes government, park representatives, biologists and others. The team was created to deal with declining populations of massasaugas in Canada.

Some of the major threats facing the massasauga include habitat loss and fragmentation, road mortality, persecution from humans and illegal collection and trade. Massasaugas relocated outside their home range will also likely die as the snakes need familiar territory to survive. Due to their small populations, massasaugas are also vulnerable to inbreeding and disease.

If you come across a massasauga on a trail or in a campground in Georgian Bay Islands National Park, report it. A park employee will collect the snake, record information about the animal and then release the reptile in the same area — but away from any facilities.

For more information on the eastern massasauga rattlesnake and to find out ways to help them, visit the Eastern Massasauga Rattlesnake Recovery Team's website: www.massasauga.ca

Releasing massassauga rattlesnakes

Lichen-covered rock on Gray Island

animals. This transition zone is known as The Land Between, an ecotone that extends from Georgian Bay in the west to the Frontenac Arch in eastern Ontario.

The soils created on limestone are different from soils on the Canadian Shield — and both are found on Beausoleil Island which is another reason for the park's rich biodiversity.

The moderating effect of Georgian Bay must also be considered when looking at the diversity of plants and animals in GBINP. This warming effect from a large body of water results in species found on the park's islands that are not found farther inland.

When you combine these factors you are left with a truly special place that is home to an abundance of plants and animals.

Georgian Bay Islands National Park is home to 33 species of reptiles and amphibians. And while the diversity of reptile species found in the park is impressive, it is concerning that approximately half are "at-risk" species. Reptiles found in the park include snakes and turtles as well as the five-lined skink – Ontario's only native lizard. Reptiles and amphibians recorded in GBINP are: Blanding's turtle, northern map turtle, midland painted turtle, snapping turtle, spotted turtle, stinkpot, DeKay's brownsnake, common gartersnake, eastern foxsnake, eastern hog-nosed snake,

Plants growing in sheltered area of Gray Island

eastern grey squirrel and the eastern chipmunk are also represented. Mammals who stick close to, or in, water include beaver, muskrat and river otter. There are also porcupine, raccoon, striped skunk, mink, snowshoe hare, long-tailed weasel, white-tailed deer, black bear, moose, coyote, red fox and fisher.

Birds are abundant with numerous species of owls, hawks, terns, gulls, ducks, woodpeckers, songbirds – and many others. Some of the at-risk species recorded in the park include the cerulean warbler, golden-winged warbler, common nighthawk, loggerhead shrike, rusty blackbird and the chimney swift. Two birds who have overcome, to varying degrees, the harmful impacts of pesticides are the osprey and the double-crested cormorant.

Numerous plant species found in the park include the impressive beech and maple forests on the southern part of Beausoleil Island to lichens clinging to rocks on the outer islands. One at-risk plant found in the park is the forked three-awned grass which grows on Beausoleil Island and nearby Christian Island – two of only five known areas in Canada where this grass is found.

More than 80 species of fish have been recorded in the eastern part of Georgian Bay with many of these species occurring in waters surrounding the park. Common species include smallmouth bass, largemouth bass, yellow perch, walleye, rock bass, black crappie, common carp and northern pike.

eastern milksnake, northern watersnake, red-bellied snake, eastern ribbonsnake, ring-necked snake, smooth greensnake, eastern massasauga rattlesnake, American toad, American bullfrog, green frog, northern leopard frog, western chorus frog, pickerel frog, spring peeper, gray treefrog, wood frog, blue-spotted salamander, four-toed salamander, eastern red-backed salamander, spotted salamander, eastern newt, five-lined skink, mudpuppy.

Resident mammals include species of moles, voles, mice and shrews. Several bat species also live in the park. The red squirrel, the

We encountered this great blue heron in Little Dog Channel on one of our park visits

ACTIVITIES

Accessible only by water, Georgian Bay Islands National Park has lots to do for boaters and sailors who want to enjoy the stunning scenery of Georgian Bay's east shore. Marinas in Honey Harbour and other communities have launching and parking areas for boaters. Park visitors with their own boats are advised to include nautical maps of the area. There are many accessible docks along the east side of Beausoleil Island. You can also access Beausoleil from the park's shuttle boat *DayTripper*, or get a private water taxi. There is also a dock on Bone Island.

Beausoleil Island is the only island in GBINP where you are allowed to camp. Campgrounds are located along the island's eastern shore and at the north end. The campground at Cedar Spring is the largest campground on Beausoleil and offers optional accommodations such as cabins and oTENTiks (a cross between a tent and a cabin). Other facilities available at Cedar Spring include a Visitor Centre, interpretive programs and a comfort station.

Cabins are also available on the island's west side at Christian Beach. And you'll also find campgrounds at Tonch Point (Tonch North has paddle-in campsites), Chimney

Bay, Thumb Point and Honeymoon Bay on the northern tip of Beausoleil.

Canoeing and kayaking are excellent ways of experiencing the rocky islands and scenic waters. But since the area is not without its dangers, those considering exploring this area by canoe or kayak should be experienced paddlers and take all of the necessary safety precautions. Open areas of the bay can produce high winds and rough waters while the more inland areas can have considerable boat traffic – especially during summer months. Since many of the boats in the park are large, paddlers often have to navigate substantial wakes. Dangers from storms that can quickly come up must also be heeded.

There is good hiking at GBINP. Only Beausoleil Island has trails and the trail system on the large island is impressive, with 12 footpaths and more than 35 kilometres of trails that cover much of the island. Some trails are under a kilometre while others, such as the Huron Trail and the Georgian Trail, are approximately seven kilometres long.

Trails on the southern part of Beausoleil take you through beautiful beech-maple forests, or allow you to visit the Cemetery of the Oak along an interpretive trail. Another trail provides sweeping views of Georgian Bay. The Georgian Trail follows the west side of the island extending from Beausoleil Point almost as far as Turtle Bay.

The northern part of the island has trails that take you past a beautiful wetland as well

YMCA camp on Beausoleil Island

as areas that provide views over Long Bay and the eastern shoreline. These trails also provide a pleasant walk over rocky terrain. The Fairy Trail is a nice, 2.9-kilometre loop that goes around Fairy Lake and Goblin Lake.

There are also trails open for cycling.

Picnicking areas also exist within the park. Beausoleil Island has a fine selection of decent picnic areas, and there is a good picnic area on Bone Island. You can dock at either one of these islands. If you can access the other islands you can explore them during the day and picnic by the Bay.

If you want to go swimming, Beausoleil Island has many places to drop a towel, with beaches along the island's eastern shore as well as in a few sheltered bays at the north end of the island. These areas are not supervised and protective footwear is recommended in some areas.

The natural beauty of the area is stunning. And its constantly changing landscapes through the seasons offer endless opportunities for the amateur and professional photographer.

For more information: www.parkscanada.gc.ca/gbi

OUR PARK ADVENTURES

Lynn and I have hiked much of Beausoleil Island, explored some of the park's other islands and traveled the waters of this special place on several occasions. However,

A wild rose on Island 176

one visit stands out when late in July we accompanied two Parks Canada employees to several areas of the park.

We set out from the park's dock in Honey Harbour in the morning. We traveled through Big Dog Channel that separates Little Beausoleil Island from Roberts Island before turning southwest and heading toward Cedar Spring on the southeast part of Beausoleil Island. Cedar Spring was our first stop and we wanted to refamiliarize ourselves with this area and see some of the changes that had taken place since our last visit here. Cedar Spring features the Visitor Centre, a boardwalk and

Cedar Spring area of Beausoleil Island

a campground. It's also where the *DayTripper* carries visitors to the park.

Walking along the boardwalk from the docks to the Visitor Centre we came across some midland painted turtles basking in the sun. Cedar Spring has several camping options from basic campsites to oTENTiks (a cross between a tent and a cabin). There are also cabins at Cedar Spring and on the west side of the island at Christian Beach.

This part of the large island also has a cemetery – Cemetery of the Oak – where First Nations people along with European immigrants and Voyageurs were buried from 1845 to 1950. It is a beautiful, peaceful spot which we have visited on several occasions. This is also the area where there was a settlement in the 1840s and the 1850s under the leadership of Chief John Assance and you can still make out some of the land where agriculture occurred. The endangered plant forked three-awned grass is also found on this part of the island.

On our way back we came across a few park projects. One includes the planting of native trees and the creation of gardens for bees and butterflies that make the area more desirable for various animals. The gardens feature such plants as milkweed and brown-eyed Susan. Quite a few protective boxes had also been placed in areas where turtle eggs might be

Canoeing in Little Dog Channel

McCabe Rock, Beausoleil Island

buried. These boxes will help protect the eggs until they have a chance to hatch. While these projects are simple to do they effectively help restore the area to a more natural habitat, assist animals like bees, monarch butterflies and turtles, and get people involved from the community in making Beausoleil Island better for all species.

After returning to the boat we headed north to McCabe Rock. This scenic area features a smooth rock shoreline and some docks. A short walk from here takes you to the Massasauga Trail, a two-kilometre footpath that extends a little past Chimney Bay. A campground is also nearby.

Our next destination was Ojibway Bay located a little north of McCabe Rock. There is a dock at this fine bay as well as a campground nearby.

Island 176 was our next stop. While Beausoleil Island is the only park island where you can camp and stay overnight, you are allowed to explore the other smaller islands in GBINP. This one is on the northwest side of Beausoleil near Lost Bay. To get there we went through Little Dog Channel and then Main Channel and proceeded around Honeymoon Bay at the northern tip of Beausoleil. We then continued on in a southwest direction skirting the big island past Payette Island where we came upon Island 176 at the outer edge of Lost Bay and a stone's throw from Beausoleil itself.

The island is one you might expect to see in a Group of Seven painting. The small, one-acre island is a good example of Canadian Shield landscape with lots of bare rock, some grasses, bushes and flowers along with some striking windswept pines.

Prickly wild roses, milkweed and sumac were some of the plants that caught our attention here. Island 176 is a particularly good island for a picnic or swim. But we were off to one of the YMCA camps on Beausoleil Island, this one located in Goblin Bay, as the park officials we were traveling with had received a call to relocate an eastern massasauga rattlesnake.

On arrival at the camp we found the snake in an enclosed box. Parks Canada staff work with selected camp counsellors training them how to capture snakes found in the camp and to hold them in capture boxes for release. The snake was efficiently transferred into another container and then transported a short distance outside the camp for release. A photo was taken of the reptile for future reference as each snake has a unique pattern from which they can be identified. When releasing massasaugas it is important not to take them too far away from their home turf as the animal's survival is dependent on knowing where to hide from predators, where to hunt and where to locate the hibernaculum – all learned locations. A

Bee and butterfly garden on Beausoleil Island

hibernaculum is an underground chamber where a snake spends the cold months in hibernation and the same hibernaculum is usually used each year.

Shortly after this snake was released another call came from another YMCA camp located on the east side of Beausoleil. We made our way to this camp via Little Dog Channel and as we entered the channel, we saw a beautiful great blue heron sitting on a dock. The statuesque bird watched us but made no effort to leave. While I have had the pleasure of observing numerous great blue herons this was the first who didn't fly off when we were in such close proximity!

This snake relocation was similar to the

Cooling off after a Beausoleil Island hike

first except that there were three massasaugas that now needed moving. A couple of hours earlier I had never seen an eastern massasauga, and now I had seen four!

Unfortunately, the release of these incredible snakes was the last stop on this excursion to Georgian Bay Islands National Park and we returned to Honey Harbour via Big Dog Channel. But what a great day!

****

The first time Lynn and I visited GBINP is one we still talk about today. It was a warm, sunny mid-August day when we set out from Honey Harbour on a tour courtesy of Parks Canada. Our first destination was Honeymoon Bay on the northern tip of Beausoleil Island. This section of island features a stunning rocky landscape with majestic white pines, a couple of sand beaches as well as two inland lakes. There is also a dock and some campsites at Honeymoon Bay. A short hike takes you to Goblin Lake and Fairy Lake.

After wandering the northern portion of the island we headed over to explore Gray Island. Gray is one of the outer islands which is located approximately 20 kilometres from Honey Harbour. This is the furthest park island from shore situated approximately six kilometres from the mainland. Being an outer island exposed to steady wind and waves, Gray is rather stark, but it sure is spectacular!

The windy, exposed side of Gray Island is pummeled by waves crashing against barren rock. The more sheltered part features plants and some animals that appear to thrive in this relatively harsh environment. Much of Gray Island features lichen-covered rock with some wildflowers and other small plants established in the more sheltered areas. Another sheltered area includes shrubs and other plants and a vernal pool. Here we caught a glimpse of some birds in the bushes as well as some frogs and a snake.

It was difficult to leave Gray Island but we had another island to visit – Island 221. Island 221 is located close to the mainland and has some beautiful rock formations.

****

A fun family outing involved Lynn and I hiking Beausoleil Island with our children Gleannan and Liam. It was another nice summer day when we walked the island. We began in the southern part of the island where large beech, maple and oak trees thrive in the relatively deep soils and hiked north on the Huron Trail and then switched to the Rockview Trail before taking the Fairy Trail. Fairy Trail provides a stunning view of Fairy Lake.

It was difficult to see the subtle changes in the land as we walked, but the difference from the beginning of the hike to the end of the walk was striking. The lush deciduous

Hiking the north end of Beausoleil Island

Big Dog Channel

forests of the southern part of the island gave way, gradually, to the rocky landscape with the windswept pines at the north end of the island. After cooling off in Georgian Bay we returned to Honey Harbour.

****

On another family day trip we made to Beausoleil Island during the summer the four of us hiked the trails near Cedar Spring and visited the Cemetery of the Oak. Near the cemetery we met an eastern hog-nosed snake, an at-risk species, on the trail. Prior to returning home we cooled off at a beach at Cedar Spring.

****

While Georgian Bay Islands National Park is popular in the summer, it is also a special place in the fall when the trees are displaying their fall finest consisting of brilliant yellows, oranges, reds and crimsons. Combined with the green of the coniferous trees and the blue of Georgian Bay the park is truly a spectacular sight. During an October outing we enjoyed the park by boat and hiked the Lookout Trail on Beausoleil Island.

We have really enjoyed our visits to GBINP and will continue to return to this picturesque park set amongst the Thirty Thousand Islands. We would like to canoe in the park and will likely do so in the fall when boat traffic is less busy compared to the summer months. We are also planning on canoeing 12 Mile Bay where there are some park islands at the mouth of the bay.

Fairy Lake on the north end of Beausoleil Island

The Tip of Point Pelee

5. POINT PELEE NATIONAL PARK

"The marsh, to him who enters it in a receptive mood, holds, besides mosquitoes and stagnation, melody, the mystery of unknown waters, and the sweetness of Nature undisturbed by man." – Charles William Beebe

Point Pelee National Park (PPNP) is one of Canada's oldest, and smallest, national parks. Located in Essex County in southwestern Ontario, the park is some 50 kilometres southeast of Windsor and marks the most southern point of mainland in Canada. Middle Island, which is part of the park, is the southernmost point of land in Canada.

Established in 1918, PPNP is Canada's ninth national park. The small, 15-square-kilometre park consists of a V-shaped spit of land that juts southward nine kilometres into the western basin of Lake Erie. It is 4.5 kilometres wide at its northern base. The park is situated in the Carolinian life zone of the St. Lawrence Lowlands natural region and features more than 400 hectares of dry land and more than 1,000 hectares of freshwater marsh.

Due to its southerly location, moderate climate, rich soils and a variety of habitats – including one of the largest Great Lakes marshes that remain – Point Pelee is

> **POINT PELEE NATIONAL PARK**
> - Recognized as an Important Bird Area, an International Butterfly Reserve, Wetland of International Significance and Dark-Sky Preserve
> - A variety of habitat including marsh, beach, savannah, swamp forest and Carolinian forest
> - Important stopover for migrating birds and butterflies

Marsh Boardwalk in early spring

renowned for its biodiversity and numerous at-risk species.

Much of the park's interior consists of the impressive marsh, the importance of which was acknowledged by the UNESCO Ramsar Convention when it designated the park in 1987 as a Wetland of International Significance. A one-kilometre-long boardwalk allows you to observe, up close, part of this incredible wetland. Other habitats include forest, beach, savannah and swamp forest.

Middle Island has been part of Point Pelee National Park since 2000. The 18.5-hectare island is part of a group of islands in the western basin of Lake Erie.

Although PPNP is primarily a day-use park, there is much to do here including hiking the park's numerous trails, bird watching, canoeing and kayaking, swimming, photography, bicycling and picnicking. The park was designated an Important Bird Area in 1998 and is also recognized as an International Butterfly Reserve. It was the first national park to be designated a Dark-Sky Preserve which it received in 2006. The park also has a fascinating human history dating back thousands of years.

PARK HISTORY

Point Pelee National Park was established in 1918. The park's creation can be attributed to

Barn swallows on Marsh Boardwalk

the migratory birds who passed through this area and the ornithologists who observed them, including Percy Taverner, William Brodie and William Saunders.[9]

W. F. Lothian, in his book *A Brief History of Canada's National Parks*, explains:

"Before the end of the (19th) century, the unusual opportunities for the study of bird and plant life began to attract the attention of naturalists. Among these were W. E. Saunders of London, Ontario, and P. A. Taverner of Ottawa, both well-known ornithologists. Conservation groups also became interested in preserving the habitat of waterfowl. In its annual report for 1915, the Commission of Conservation at Ottawa published a report by Taverner, recommending the creation of a national park at Point Pelee."

Before this, Point Pelee's human history stretched back thousands of years to when First Nations peoples camped and hunted on the peninsula. The peninsula eventually got its current name from the French who landed here. Pelée means "bald" or "bare" and was in reference to the point's sparse vegetation.

In 1670, Jesuit priests Fathers Dollier and Galinée explored the area while camping on Point Pelee. In the late 1790s, in order to protect the tall, straight trees – particularly the white pine – that grew on the Pelee Peninsula, the

British created a naval reserve on what is now Point Pelee National Park.

Point Pelee also played a part in the War of 1812 as General Brock and his expedition camped on its shores in 1812. Previously, a band of Pottawatomi (now called the Caldwell First Nation) lived at Point Pelee. The Caldwell Band was promised a homeland at Point Pelee by Brock for their loyal military service during the War, but he died before his promise was fulfilled.

During the late 1800s, government officials forced the Caldwell Band to leave Point Pelee. Some members of the Caldwell First Nation continued to live at Point Pelee until the 1920s. Those who returned were again forced out in 1922 by the RCMP. An interpretive sign in the park notes that the RCMP hoped to keep members of the Caldwell First Nation away by "destroying their root cellars to ensure they wouldn't return."

Settlement of the British naval reserve began in the early 1830s with the arrival of a handful of families. These "squatters," also known as "Pointers," formed the first European settlement here. They fished, hunted, grew vegetables and fruit and kept cattle and pigs who were allowed to roam, destroying much of the fragile natural habitat. Trapping, logging and sand and gravel removal further impacted the area.

According to Henrietta O'Neill's *In Search of a Heart*, settlers were not hospitable to Native

Mourning Cloak Butterfly

Peoples who were also farming here. "They jealously guarded their small holdings," she noted, "and worked ruthlessly to drive out the original native inhabitants, who also were farming."

Fishing for sustenance soon gave way to commercialized fishing along these shores and it didn't take long before fish populations suffered. O'Neill explains:

"As fishing became more commercialized and demand increased, pound nets came into use followed by gill nets. By 1855 fishermen were exporting their catch to the United States and by 1861 even the lowly sturgeon had found its niche in the marketplace. European immigrants had established a sturgeon

DeLaurier Homestead

fishery on the peninsula and were selling its oil in Detroit for 75 cents a gallon. In 1872, the government sought to control fishing by dividing the shoreline into water lots that were leased to the fisheries. By 1891 the Point Pelee shoreline was blanketed by 22 licences. Nine years later, sturgeon had been nearly eliminated and lake trout, whitefish and lake herring populations had also declined."

In 1871, the Point Pelee Naval Reserve was transferred by the British Admiralty to Canada. In 1891, families that had formerly squatted on the former Naval Reserve were given free title to the land they had been living on. Such families included the DeLauriers, Abbots and LeFleurs.

Generations of DeLauriers have lived at Point Pelee since 1832.[10] The classic DeLaurier House log cabin was built by Oliver and Esther DeLaurier between 1851 and 1861. Their grandson, Roy DeLaurier, lived in this house for some 70 years. Roy's brother, Ed DeLaurier, was the last of the DeLauriers to live here which he did until 1969 when Parks Canada assumed title.

This historic building is the only remaining structure in the park built in the 19th century and along with the barn, is a fine representative example of the small community buildings that existed here between 1850 and the late 1960s.

At one time, the community here included a number of houses, cottages, several shops, a couple of hotels and even a post office and lighthouse.

Since its creation in 1918, Point Pelee National Park attracted considerable use by visitors who came to camp, cottage, picnic or use the beaches. The invention of the automobile and improved roads was responsible for much of this activity. W. F. Lothian describes the national park's early decades in *A Brief History of Canada's National Parks*:

"As the park's attractions became better known, visitor use increased and, by 1925, the annual attendance was estimated to be 50,000 ...Unfortunately, much of the best land in the park was privately owned, for 30 years earlier, 212 ha had been Crown-granted to the squatters. As visitor use of the park increased, property-owners began to sell portions of their land, and many of the original lots were subdivided for cottage sites. Eventually, privately-owned property in the park was owned by several hundred persons, many of them residents of the United States."

In fact, cottage development in Point Pelee continued well into the 1960s.

Even during the Great Depression the park remained extremely popular. Henrietta O'Neill explains:

"During the Great Depression, the cities of Detroit and Windsor emptied their unemployed into Point Pelee. Families moved in bag and baggage, leaving only the breadwinner (usually the father) in the city to work. Here, two dollars would get a months' rent, food was readily available and recreation for the children was right at their door step, or more accurately, tent flap."

Beach near the Tip

As the popularity grew, park officials designated specific areas for camping, picnicking and swimming, and associated facilities were built to accommodate these activities. The popularity of the park continued to increase. According to Parks Canada there were 781,000 visitors in 1963.[11]

Not surprisingly, all this impacted the natural environment. Much land was cleared, animal species were extirpated and non-native

POINT PELEE NATIONAL PARK

Dark skies at Point Pelee National Park Photo: © Parks Canada plant species were introduced. Contaminants such as DDT were also released. Early attempts to help reduce such impacts are described in *In Search of a Heart*.

"Camping was consolidated into one large campground in 1951, and four large parking lots were built to accommodate tourists. An intensive program of land acquisition went into effect in 1956, and by 1970, all but 80 acres belonged to the Park. Bill Gallacher, superintendent, introduced a new plan for Point Pelee in 1971. In May of that year, only 55 of the 152 campsites opened; a transit system obtained from Expo '67 carried visitors to the Tip from the Visitor Centre; and the refreshment stand on East Point Beach closed permanently."

The park continued its efforts to reduce the human footprint in the latter half of the 20th century. According to "Point Pelee National Park of Canada State of the Park Report 2006," Parks Canada restored close to two square kilometres of land increasing the terrestrial ecosystem significantly between 1959 and 2000.[12]

Farming in the park was also stopped in the late 1960s. Many farmers had created drainage and irrigation canals many of which have been filled in by Parks Canada, although some remain providing habitat for a variety of plants and animals.

Besides significantly reducing the human footprint, other issues that have been addressed

A replica of the park's original sign leading to the DeLaurier Homestead & Trail

in PPNP include at-risk species, non-native invasive plants and habitat restoration. The southern flying squirrel, for instance, was extirpated from the park in the 1930s or 1940s and a reintroduction program, which has been successful to date, was initiated in 1993-94.

Habitat restoration is also occurring in the park. Savannah is being restored to help numerous species including the at-risk five-lined skink, yellow-breasted chat, monarch butterfly and the eastern prickly pear cactus.

Another program involves preserving the at-risk red mulberry tree. Deforestation and the spread of the non-native white mulberry tree, which can interbreed with the red, are two reasons for the red mulberry's at-risk status.

We met this wild male turkey when we visited the cemetery

A small number of red mulberry can be found on the park's mainland property as well as on Middle Island.

The 18.5-hectare Middle Island, the southernmost piece of land in Canada, was also added to Point Pelee National Park in 2000.

In 2006 PPNP was designated a Dark-Sky Preserve. Preserving the night sky is important for all species and an essential goal for parks that have a mandate of protecting animals and biodiversity.

HABITATS

When you arrive at PPNP you'll readily discover signature park habitats such as marsh, beach and a lush deciduous forest. And when you have a chance to explore the park and its rich biodiversity a little more, you will also find fascinating and important savannah and swamp forest habitats.

While PPNP has undergone considerable human disturbance, it surprisingly still contains an extraordinary Carolinian forest, something in heavy decline in Southern Ontario. This forest is home to many plants and animals including many at-risk species. The forest also features many tree species usually associated with areas farther south in the United States. Some such species include hackberry, chinquapin oak, red mulberry and sassafras. In

Swamp forest on the Woodland Nature Trail

the mature, dense forest you will also see vines clinging to many trees. A diversity of flowering plants lives on the forest floor. Trees that are more indicative of central Ontario's mixed-wood forests, including species of oak as well as sugar maple, and even white pine, can be found in the northern areas of the park.

A swamp forest also exists in the park. It's located south of the marsh. Several decades ago white elm was common here but Dutch elm disease killed much of the elm population. Flooding and storms caused further damage. Today silver maple and sycamore live in this swamp forest.

Dead trees in this forest provide nesting sites for a variety of birds including wrens, woodpeckers, tree swallows and even the prothonotary warbler; PPNP is one of a few nesting sites in Ontario for this warbler who, according to Parks Canada, likes to nest in rotting stumps in swamp forests.

The marsh is the largest habitat in PPNP with wetlands covering approximately two-thirds of the park. This Great Lakes marsh is one of the largest remaining marshes in Southern Ontario. Because of its size and importance, this wetland was designated a UNESCO Wetland of International Significance in 1987. The marsh consists largely of cattails, along with less conspicuous plants, that enclose numerous ponds including Lake Pond, West Cranberry Pond, East Cranberry Pond, Redhead Pond and Girardin Pond. A variety of reptiles, amphibians, mammals, birds and fishes live in and around the marsh and its ponds.

The PPNP beach is a popular habitat. It covers approximately 20 kilometres of shoreline along the east and west sides of the peninsula. This constantly changing area is battered by waves, covered in snow and ice during winter and scorched during hot summer months. The sand can reach temperatures in excess of 45°C!

While a beach might not sound like the most hospitable place to anything but sunbathers, it is home to many plants and animals, including many insects and birds. Most beach vegetation comes in the form of grasses, but an at-risk species of tree – the eastern hoptree – can also be found here. Hoptrees do well in the harsh beach environment where they grow in the hot, nutrient-poor soil. Found as far south as Mexico, the hoptree's northern range extends to southwestern Ontario. Hoptrees are a member of the citrus family and one of two main food plants used by the giant swallowtail – Canada's largest butterfly. Hoptree populations exist on the park's mainland property as well as on Middle Island.

The beach here has experienced much change over the years. According to a Parks Canada report, "The total beach area declined from 88 to 41 hectares between 1931 and 2000."[13] Deposition and erosion are natural processes in a beach habitat but human activities, including the extraction of sand and gravel, has had significant impacts

Marsh Boardwalk in late spring

Rocks on the beach near the Tip

on the shore. Henrietta O'Neill's *In Search of a Heart* notes that by the 1870s sand and gravel were being extracted from the point for construction in the United States. She also notes that there was serious erosion at Pelee's tip due to off-shore removal of sand by dredges and that by 1905, the tip had receded by at least one-half mile.

In the years leading up to establishment of PPNP, until a couple of years after the park's creation, federal permits allowed removal of sand and gravel from park beaches, including at the tip of Point Pelee. Provincial authorization also allowed lake-bottom dredging for much of the 20th century.

Besides human activities, natural processes also bring significant change to the park's beaches. This alteration in the beach habitat is very noticeable at the tip which can change significantly in both shape and length due to many factors, especially winds and wave action.

Savannah is another important habitat in the park, and home to approximately 25% of the park's species at risk. Savannah is an early successional habitat that features few trees, but a good diversity of grasses, wildflowers and other plants. Red cedar is found here along with the rare eastern prickly pear cactus. Butterflies and the endangered five-lined skink also live in savannah habitat within the park.

PPNP savannah is divided into two habitat types – beach and old field. Beach savannah is found inland from the open beach while old field savannah occurs at former cottage sites and abandoned farms. Restoring savannah is a priority within Parks Canada; although savannah habitat represents a small portion of the park, it contains many of the at-risk species found here. Approximately a dozen savannah habitat restoration sites have been identified in various parts of the park. Restoration activities include planting native plants, removing invasive and exotic species and conducting prescribed burns which help eliminate exotic plant species.

GEOLOGY

Point Pelee is a spit of land that extends into Lake Erie. This sandspit is really a layer of sediment 60 metres or thicker that sits atop 300-million-year-old sedimentary bedrock. Sediments covering this bedrock include sand, clay, silt and gravel. These sediments were left in the area by the advancing and retreating glaciers that covered Southern Ontario starting more than a million years ago.

The last ice age ended about 12,000 years ago. As the glacier melted, large lakes appeared then receded somewhat, leaving behind beaches, bars and spits. Waves created by winds and currents also eroded shores and

Deciduous trees reflecting on the water next to the Woodland Nature Trail

transported the sand and gravel to help form the peninsula.

FLORA & FAUNA

Point Pelee National Park has a rich diversity of plants and animals. There are various reasons for this biodiversity including the park's location and climate. The park is located in the Carolinian life zone of the St. Lawrence Lowlands natural region and it shares the same latitude as northern California. This is the most southerly zone in this region and, according to Parks Canada, "the most species-rich in Canada" as well.[14]

The Carolinian life zone begins in the

Red admiral butterfly

Carolinas and spreads north between the Appalachian Mountains and the Mississippi River into southwestern Ontario. In Ontario, this zone extends from the north shore of Lake Ontario to the south shore of Lake Huron, south to the southernmost area of the province which includes Middle Island in Lake Erie. While this zone (also known as "Carolinian Canada" and the eastern deciduous forest) has an incredible biodiversity, it makes up less than 1% of the land area in Canada. For many species, Carolinian Canada is the northern limit of their range.

Besides its southern latitude, the park's moderate climate is also related to the fact that it is almost completely surrounded by Lake Erie, and sits in relative close proximity to the other Great Lakes as well. Since water temperatures change more slowly than land temperatures, the heat that the lakes acquire during the summer months is released slowly, resulting in a warmer fall and winter. This "lake effect" provides the Carolinian life zone with a warmer winter than areas with a similar latitude, but without the moderating effects of the Great Lakes.

Habitats in the park also contribute to its rich flora and fauna. Marsh, Carolinian forest, savannah, swamp forest and beach provide homes and shelter for numerous plants and animals. The area's rich soils also contribute to its biodiversity.

Extending well out into Lake Erie, this spit of land is also an important staging area for migratory birds and insects such as the monarch butterfly. While numerous bird species do nest and live here, the majority of the more than 390 bird species that arrive at Point Pelee use the park as a stopover destination during migration. Point Pelee National Park is situated along both the Mississippi and Atlantic flyways and with its variety of habitats is a welcome and accommodating resting area for birds. Indeed, the park forms a natural and helpful migration corridor across the lake for these birds.

Although PPNP is known for its beautiful Carolinian forest, it's the birds who now attract so many people to Canada's southernmost point of land. And we have early ornithologists such as Percy Taverner, William Brodie, William Saunders and others to thank as they were early supporters of the park.[15]

While the Carolinian life zone has a rich diversity of species, it is also home to a large number of at-risk bird species such as the eastern wood-peewee, eastern whip-poor-will, bobolink, peregrine falcon, short-eared owl, barn swallow, eastern meadowlark, wood thrush, cerulean warbler, red-headed woodpecker, prothonotary warbler, piping

Indigo bunting

DESIGNATIONS OF POINT PELEE NATIONAL PARK

In a 2006 report, Parks Canada points out how less than 6% of PPNP is forested and how most of the region's wetlands have been destroyed. As much as 50% of this area was once occupied by wetlands and today less than 3% remains. The significant wetland that remains in PPNP was recognized in 1987 when the UNESCO Ramsar Convention designated the park a Wetland of International Significance.

Point Pelee National Park's importance to butterflies was also acknowledged when the park was declared an International Butterfly Reserve. From late August into the middle of October monarch butterflies pass through the park on their more than 4,000-kilometre journey to Mexico.

In 1998, PPNP was then designated an Important Bird Area. With more than 390 bird species sighted here, this designation certainly is appropriate. The park provides good nesting sites for numerous species of birds and its location along two flyways provides a critical staging area for migrating birds.

Then in 2006, PPNP was designated a Dark-Sky Preserve. Dark night skies are important for protecting the nocturnal habitat of animals such as birds, bats, insects and amphibians.

Canal on the DeLaurier Homestead & Trail

Female red-winged blackbird

plover, least bittern, hooded warbler, Henslow's sparrow, chimney swift, Canada warbler, and loggerhead shrike.

One bird found in large numbers in the park, particularly on Middle Island, is the double-crested cormorant. This native species is a migratory waterbird who consumes fish and nests in colonies. During the 1970s, the number of these birds in the Great Lakes declined significantly, largely due to pesticide use. Populations of double-crested cormorants have since recovered and these birds now nest in large numbers on some of the islands in western Lake Erie.

Middle Island is one spot where double-crested cormorants nest in large numbers. From the late 1980s until 2000, the number of double-crested cormorant nests on Middle Island increased from a few nests to thousands of nests. There are also colonies of other bird species on the island, including species of gulls and herons, but their numbers are significantly lower.

Nesting double-crested cormorants have posed a threat to Middle Island trees and vegetation. Parks Canada has subsequently had large numbers of these birds killed in an attempt to reduce the impacts, especially to some at-risk species such as red mulberry, Kentucky coffee-tree and the hoptree.

Dunlins (front) and black-bellied plovers (back)

White-crowned sparrow (front) and white-throated sparrow (back)

Cormorants were almost extirpated from much of the Great Lakes during the 1960s and early 1970s. Their return to the island is part of the natural process and the healthy populations of these striking native birds should be celebrated.

With so much marsh it is not surprising that numerous reptiles and amphibians have been recorded here. Unfortunately, some species have become extirpated including the gray treefrog, Blanchard's cricket frog and Fowler's toad. Some amphibians who can still be found in PPNP are the northern leopard frog, spring peeper, green frog and American toad.

Reptiles in the park include the at-risk five-lined skink along with several species of snakes and turtles including Blanding's turtle, eastern musk turtle, spiny softshell, spotted turtle, northern map turtle, snapping turtle, eastern foxsnake, northern watersnake, DeKay's brownsnake and the eastern gartersnake.

While many species of snakes once lived at Point Pelee, only four are commonly found here including the eastern foxsnake. In Ontario the eastern foxsnake lives in two areas – the Carolinian Forest region, including PPNP, and the eastern side of Georgian Bay. Foxsnakes, who resemble massasauga rattlesnakes, are a species at risk, due mainly to habitat loss, human persecution, collection for the pet trade and road mortality.

Some mammals found in PPNP include raccoons, beavers, muskrats, eastern grey squirrels, eastern cottontail rabbits and coyotes. Three at-risk mammal species in the park are the eastern mole along with two species of bats – the little brown bat and the northern long-eared bat.

Like the double-crested cormorants on Middle Island, the white-tailed deer population in the park can become large, in part due to a lack of predators. In order to protect the plants in the park, deer are killed when their populations are deemed excessive.

One mammal making a comeback at Point Pelee National Park is the southern flying squirrel. This species was extirpated in the 1930s or 1940s, but reintroduction attempts have since proved successful.

Point Pelee National Park is home to a host of insects including various species of dragonflies, damselflies, spiders and butterflies. The monarch butterfly is a popular attraction in the park. In 1995, PPNP was declared a Monarch Butterfly Reserve. Some park efforts to help this species at-risk involve restoring the park's savannah habitat, including the planting of milkweed on which the Monarch exclusively lays her eggs.

Red-winged blackbird

Midland painted turtles enjoying the sunshine

A variety of fish species inhabit the park's marsh ponds including bowfin, pumpkinseed, carp and perch. Some of the at-risk fish species in PPNP are spotted gar, grass pickerel, lake chubsucker and warmouth.

As you would expect, there is an impressive diversity of plants and trees found in PPNP with its Carolinian forest, savannah, marsh and other habitats. Not only are there many species found here that are not common in the rest of Canada, but there is a large number of at-risk species as well. In fact, there are more rare species of plants found in Carolinian Canada, which has more than 70 species of trees, than in any other region in Canada.

Within the park itself there are numerous species of at-risk trees including red mulberry, dwarf hackberry, hoptree and the Kentucky coffee-tree. Native to the Carolinian forest are hackberry trees and there are two species within PPNP – dwarf hackberry and the northern hackberry. The fruit of these trees provides food for various animals including squirrels and birds. Caterpillars of the hackberry emperor butterfly, tawny emperor butterfly and American snout butterfly depend on these trees for food.

The spicebush is another important park plant. The spicebush swallowtail butterfly lays its eggs on its leaves. When the eggs hatch the

THE IMPORTANCE OF WETLANDS

Wetlands are some of the most important and productive places on the planet. Here in Ontario we are fortunate to have approximately a quarter of Canada's wetlands and 6% of the world's wetlands. Wetlands in Ontario include marshes, swamps, fens, bogs and shallow open water.

Unfortunately, here in Southern Ontario people have destroyed the vast majority – up to 80% or more – of pre-settlement wetlands. This staggering amount increases to more than 90% in parts of southwestern Ontario, making places like the PPNP marsh all the more valuable.

Why are wetlands so important? For starters, they perform a myriad of pivotal roles. They provide vital habitat to many species of plants, birds, amphibians, reptiles, mammals, fishes and invertebrates. The health of the environment is associated with biodiversity so wetlands are important in maintaining a healthy environment.

Another important wetland function is water purification. Wetlands purify water by removing contaminants, suspended particles and excessive nutrients.

Flood control is another task performed by wetlands which act as reservoirs soaking up excess water which is then slowly released during drier seasons. Not only does this help control flooding, it also reduces soil erosion and the effects of drought.

Wetlands also help out with global warming by providing oxygen while retaining carbon from decaying plants and animals.

Not to be overlooked is the importance of

The vast majority of wetlands in Southern Ontario have been destroyed

wetlands for recreational opportunities such as canoeing, kayaking, hiking and bird watching.

Every time we damage or destroy a wetland we are harming the health of the environment, increasing the likelihood of flooding and reducing the quality of the water.

Cemetery

caterpillars' food source is right before them.

Other tree species found in the park include American sycamore, swamp white oak, blue ash and sassafras. The fruit of the sassafras tree provides food for many birds and mammals while the foliage of these trees is consumed by some caterpillars. In Canada, sassafras trees are only naturally found along Lake Erie's north shore. They grow in several areas of the park. The American sycamore is one of the larger tree species in PPNP and it can be found in the park's swamp forest.

Point Pelee National Park is also home to many plant species such as horsetail, Dutchman's breeches, may-apple, bloodroot and woodland sunflower. The park's Carolinian forest also contains vines from plants such as wild grape and Virginia creeper, which climb through trees reaching for sunlight.

The park savannah is also home to a variety of plants. One at-risk plant that lives in this habitat is the eastern prickly pear cactus. This plant grows naturally in PPNP and on Pelee Island, the only known such locations in Canada.

ACTIVITIES

Many people associate Point Pelee with bird watching – and for good reason. This sand spit that extends approximately nine kilometres into Lake Erie is an important stopover for migrating birds, giving bird watchers a wonderful opportunity to observe, and photograph, any of the more than 390 species known to have lived in, or passed through, the park.

PPNP is one of the best locations in North America to watch the spring bird migration which occurs from March to June. Ducks, geese, swans, loons and other waterbirds arrive in March. The spring songbird migration begins in April and the first few weeks of May is a particularly good time to see songbirds – something that attracts bird watchers from all over North America – and beyond!

The park is renowned for its spring warbler migration. According to Parks Canada, 43 warbler species have been recorded at PPNP with 39 warbler species having been observed in just one migration. Incredibly, 34 species of warblers were seen by one person in a single day!

June in the park brings shorebirds and flycatchers. The spring migration is so popular at Point Pelee that the park now holds a "Festival of Birds" in May.

The fall migration is also excellent. Songbirds appear in August while September brings birds of prey including sharp-shinned hawks and Cooper's hawks. October brings others such as peregrine falcons and majestic golden eagles. Many birds of prey follow Lake Erie's shoreline which funnels many birds right into the park. November calls some waterbirds such as geese and diving ducks, including red-breasted and common mergansers as well as greater and lesser scaups.

Centennial Bike & Hike Trail

Bird watching doesn't have to be limited to just the park either. Nearby Hillman Marsh Conservation Area and Pelee Island offer good bird watching opportunities as well.

Monarch butterflies also migrate through the park in fall as part of their more than 4,000-kilometre journey to Mexico. These butterflies cross the Great Lakes at the narrowest points, including Point Pelee. Monarch butterflies migrate through Ontario between late August and October.

PPNP is a wonderful spot for a walk in the

Woodland Trail

woods...or savannah, or beach, or marsh. The park's many footpaths allow access to these beautiful places.

A good place to start is at the Tip of Point Pelee – the most southern point of mainland Canada. From spring until fall there is a shuttle that takes you from the Visitor Centre close to the Tip which you can then access via the Tip Trail, a one-kilometre-long loop trail. The Tip and beach shorelines that extend back from the Tip are special places. Due to the dangerous currents here there is no swimming or wading. The Tip is a good spot to observe migrating birds in spring as well as dragonflies and monarch butterflies in fall.

South of the Visitor Centre is the picturesque Woodland Nature Trail. The slightly less than three-kilometre-long loop allows you to visit the park's incredible Carolinian forest. The swamps along this trail are particularly scenic.

Another one-kilometre-long loop is the Tilden Woods Trail located just north of the Visitor Centre. This trail provides access to mature swamp forest and cedar savannah habitats.

A longer loop is the Chinquapin Oak Trail. This four-kilometre-long loop is accessible from the Tilden Woods Trail. Here you'll see mixed dry forest including the southern tree species, the chinquapin oak.

The DeLaurier Homestead & Trail includes interpretive signs so you can learn about the area's human history. It's a loop trail slightly over a kilometre long. You will learn about First Nations peoples who have lived here going back thousands of years, and something about the first settlers, including the DeLauriers, who arrived in the 1830s. Part of the history here includes the DeLaurier house and barn. A short loop trail takes you to the house and barn while the longer loop trail takes you past old fields and irrigation canals. The house, which was originally built in the mid-1800s, provides a glimpse into Canada's homesteading past.

Another short one is Shuster Trail. This half-kilometre-long trail starts at the Tilden Woods Trail and goes to the Eastern Barrier Beach.

If you enjoy wetlands there is the Marsh Boardwalk in the northern part of the park. This impressive boardwalk trail is an approximately one-kilometre-long loop that extends into the park's beautiful marsh. Before you start this hike you can climb the observation tower for a look out over the cattail marsh. Along the footpath into the marsh keep an eye out for birds, turtles, fishes and other animals. Don't forget your binoculars.

If you want a longer walk — or to bicycle ride — there is the six-kilometre-long Bike & Hike Trail that starts just south of the park entrance and runs to the Visitor Centre. This trail takes you through savannah, beach and forest.

Since the majority of PPNP is marsh, there is lots of park to explore by canoe or kayak. You can launch at the Marsh Boardwalk or rent a canoe here. Once you have paddled through Thiessen Channel there are various connected ponds you can explore at leisure.

When you need some time to rest, or have something to eat, there are picnic areas and shelters throughout PPNP. There are also swimming areas at a few of the beaches on the west side of the park.

If you want to stay longer than a day, there are oTENTik (a cross between a tent and a rustic cabin) accommodations available.

Yellow warbler

FRIENDS OF POINT PELEE

When you arrive at PPNP chances are you will enjoy something provided by Friends of Point Pelee. Established in 1981, Friends of Point Pelee is a charitable, not-for-profit organization created to support the park.

Its mandate includes providing services and resources as well as assisting with research, education and habitat restoration. Some services provided by this association include partnering with the park to present the Festival of Birds event and operating the gift store at the Visitor Centre.

If you are looking to rent a canoe you can get one from Friends of Point Pelee at the Marsh Boardwalk. The money raised is used for their operations and to support park initiatives.

Creating literature and exhibits and hosting guided hikes are some of the organization's other contributions. The Friends has also contributed to savannah habitat restoration in the park.

For more information on Friends of Point Pelee visit: http://friendsofpointpelee.com

PPNP also has exceptional opportunities for photographers. Not only is the scenery beautiful and the diversity of plants and animals incredible, there are great spots from which to take photos, including more than 15 kilometres of trails and footpaths along with beaches and a couple of lookouts.

For more information: www.parkscanada.gc.ca/pelee

OUR PARK ADVENTURES

I had heard about what a special place Point Pelee was, but I had never been there. That changed when Lynn and I arrived here mid June. We parked and caught the shuttle at the Visitor Centre which took us to an exhibit area located near the Tip. From there we took a short trail east to the shore of Lake Erie where we were greeted by noisy birds. One avian altercation featured a red-winged blackbird and a turkey vulture. The view here was spectacular with all the birds, the waves crashing on the shore and the forest inland.

Lynn and I reached the Tip by walking along the beach. The Tip is mainland Canada's

Black tern near Marsh Boardwalk

most southern point and many people had gathered here for that reason alone, and maybe to enjoy the view and take photographs. The length and shape of this sandy spit can change significantly in a short period. It won't be the same the next time you visit.

After taking the shuttle back to the Visitor Centre we set off on the three-kilometre Woodland Nature Trail located near the Visitor Centre. This scenic loop takes you through the oldest forest in the park. Interpretive signs inform the hiker about especially fascinating trees in this Carolinian forest which contains black walnut, white ash, northern hackberry, shagbark hickory, silver maple and sassafras.

After checking out the rustic DeLaurier house we decided to hit the Marsh Boardwalk. We began by ascending the observation tower that looks out over the extensive marsh and ponds. This marsh is recognized as a Ramsar Wetland of International Significance. The view from this elevated spot was awesome and consisted of a sea of cattails, lily pads and other wetland plants along with some open water and a floating boardwalk. The one-kilometre boardwalk allows you access into the wondrous wetland and the incredible animals who live here.

****

Our next visit to Point Pelee National Park occurred approximately 11 months later when we arrived on Mother's Day in May. We had set off from home before 7 a.m. arriving at the park just before 11 a.m. While the drive to PPNP is fairly long for us, it is surprising how much you can see on one of these day trips.

It was sunny and relatively warm when we began our day's activities at the Visitor Centre. This area was busier than the last time we were here. Not only was it Mother's Day, but the Festival of Birds was on too. Some birdwatchers had been in the park as early as 5 a.m.

From here we took the short Shuster Trail to the East Barrier Beach. This half-kilometre-long trail was quiet as most park visitors were on the longer trails. Lynn and I passed through dramatic woods and wetlands. Making time to walk this short trail was well worth it and a good reminder that often the shorter paths less travelled are the ones worth taking! Here we saw lots of birds including yellow warblers, tree swallows and Baltimore orioles.

Next on our hiking agenda was the Woodland Nature Trail. Here we saw black-and-white warblers and the incredible forest where many trees were just beginning to come out in leaf.

Next was White Pine where we hit the beach located on the west side of the peninsula between Black Willow Beach and West Beach. The Centennial Bike & Hike Trail runs past this site and extends along the west side of the park from near the Visitor Centre in the south to approximately Northwest Beach in the north.

Located across the road from White Pine was a cemetery, our next destination. We accessed it along a footpath. The cemetery is located in a beautiful setting – and is one of the most scenic cemeteries that I've seen. Here we saw both white-crowned sparrows and white-throated sparrows. We then decided to head over to the marsh. Our departure, however, was delayed by a large wild male turkey loitering near the cemetery's entrance. Not wanting to disturb the regal bird we sat still for the next 10 minutes admiring him.

Our final activity this day was a canoe trip into the marsh. We headed out from the docks at the Marsh Services Canoe Rental through Thiessen Channel and into Lake Pond where we explored a couple of intimate bays. Birds abounded, including black-bellied plovers and dunlins. We were also treated to a bald eagle soaring high overhead. At the same time swallows swooped by near our canoe. The relaxing paddle in this fascinating wetland was an ideal way to end our visit to Point Pelee National Park.

Beach at White Pine

Little Rouge Creek in fall as seen from the Vista Trail

6. ROUGE NATIONAL URBAN PARK

"The long fight to save wild beauty represents democracy at its best. It requires citizens to practice the hardest of virtues – self-restraint." – Edwin Way Teale

Rouge National Urban Park (RNUP) is Canada's first national urban park. While the word "urban" is usually associated with cities, highways and high population densities, this park is primarily rural and has lots of "wild" elements to it. It is also large! The Government of Canada nearly doubled the already vast urban park by more than 39 square kilometres bringing the size of Rouge to a little more than 79 square kilometres.

The park extends from Rouge Beach and Marsh on Lake Ontario in the south to the Township of Uxbridge in the north. It includes the cities of Toronto, Markham and Pickering. These lands feature a variety of habitats including meadows, wetlands, forests and beach. Large tracts of farmland are also contained within the park which protects the watersheds of the Rouge River, Petticoat Creek and Duffins Creek.

The Rouge is an exciting addition to Parks Canada for a variety of reasons including its proximity to

ROUGE NATIONAL URBAN PARK
- Canada's first national urban park
- Accessible by public transit
- Home to more than 1,700 species of plants and animals
- Approximately 22 times larger than New York's Central Park
- Rare Carolinian habitat

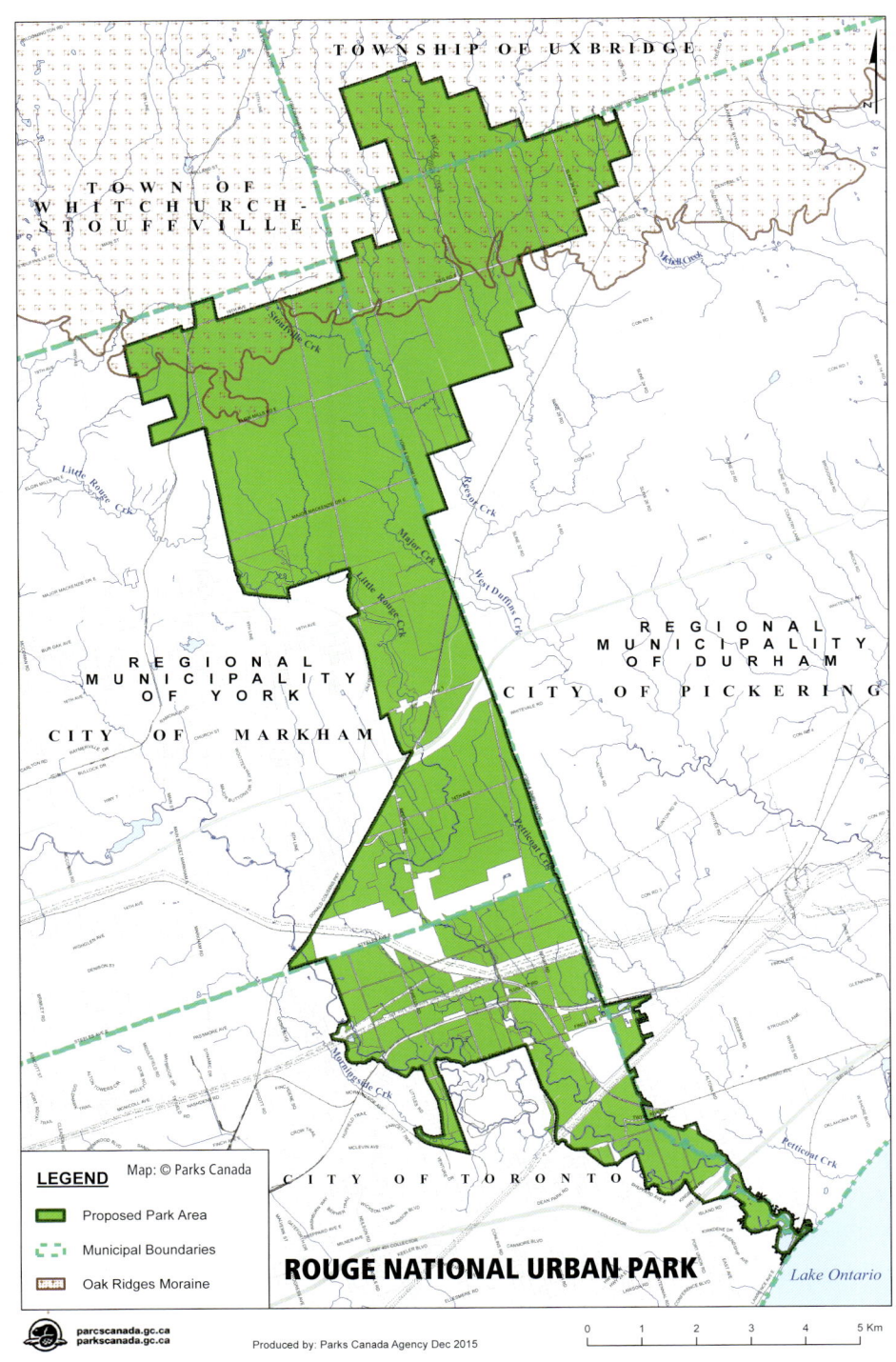

Rouge National Urban Park has a variety of wetlands

Canada's largest city. Approximately 20% of Canada's population lives near this urban park. Located in the Greater Toronto Area (GTA), parts of RNUP are accessible by public transit, thereby providing access to a national park to people who might not normally be able to visit one. With this access comes valuable nature opportunities.

According to Parks Canada, more than 1,700 species of plants and animals can be found within RNUP. Hiking, canoeing, kayaking, picnicking, photography, bird watching, cycling and camping are some of the recreational pursuits that await visitors. In winter there is also hiking, cross-country skiing and snowshoeing.

The size of Rouge National Urban Park is impressive. At over 79 square kilometres, RNUP is approximately 22 times bigger than Central Park in New York. And there is no shortage of things to do and see here.

PARK HISTORY

RNUP was established under federal stewardship in 2015, while the former Rouge Park had been established by the Province of Ontario in 1995. The area that makes up this urban park has a fascinating history extending back thousands of years. After the last glacier retreated from the region approximately 12,000 years ago, the area's forests, rivers, streams, valleys and wetlands

Rouge River in Fall

became home to people as well as to many species of plants and animals.

The first humans here were nomadic hunters who followed animals like caribou. Later, First Nations peoples turned to fishing and farming and living in more permanent houses and villages within the Rouge Watershed. Canoes were used for travel. In the mid to late 17th century, a large Seneca Village was located near where the Rouge River meets Little Rouge Creek. This village was home to hundreds of people. An archaeological site with remains of the village are part of Bead Hill which was designated a national historic site.

The first Europeans to set up residence in the Toronto area were two Sulpician priests from Montreal, fathers Fénelon and d'Urfé, who established a mission in 1669 at the foot of the Rouge River arm of the Toronto Carrying Place trail. The Rouge River branch of the Toronto Carrying Place trail was also designated a national historic event. The trail that was created by First Nations peoples, and used by fur traders, went along the Rouge River to the Holland River linking Lake Ontario to Lake Simcoe.

Early European settlement in the Rouge Watershed included some German settlers who were given land in the Markham area. In exchange, the settlers agreed to clear some farmland and open road access to Yonge Street.

During the early 1800s settlers cleared the land and grew some wheat. Forests of oak and pine were also felled for their valued timber. A variety of mills were established on the Rouge River and by the middle of the 19th century, sawmills, grist mills and woollen mills existed on the Rouge River and its tributaries.

Cottages were established along the lower part of the Rouge River in the latter half of the 19th century and into the 20th century. This was a time when the region started to be used for recreation.

While parts of the Rouge River area saw significant increases in population during the 20th century, much of the region has retained its agricultural land. In fact this farmland is some of the best in Canada and it continues to be farmed today. Farmland within Rouge

Canoeing the Rouge River

BOB HUNTER MEMORIAL PARK

A wonderful part of Rouge National Urban Park is the Bob Hunter Memorial Park. Located in the northern part of RNUP in the Cedar Grove Community in eastern Markham, Bob Hunter Memorial is situated just north of Steeles Avenue and west of Reesor Road. The 192-hectare-park honours Robert Hunter who was a writer, an environmental activist and a founder of Greenpeace.

The scenic park is a gateway into RNUP and restoration projects have returned much of the land to a more natural state. Wetland restoration is a significant goal here and some of the former wetlands have been re-established. The majority of wetlands in Southern Ontario have been drained or filled for farmland or land development. These short-sighted projects have resulted in the loss of incredibly productive and vital ecosystems. Wetlands are not only important for biodiversity, providing homes for many plants and animals, but they also purify water, control flooding and are a source of oxygen. Wetlands also help out with global warming by retaining carbon.

Along with the work done on the wetlands in the park, significant efforts have also been made to restore meadows, grasslands and forests through the planting of native wildflowers, grasses, shrubs and trees. The restored areas will provide homes, food and shelter for many species. Since 2015, Parks Canada and farmers in RNUP have restored more than 30 hectares of wetland and riparian habitat, 20 hectares of forest habitat and more than three kilometres of stream bank. These projects have involved the planting of more than 38,000 native trees and shrubs along with the installation of habitat structures such as raptor poles, basking logs, stones and salamander boards.

People can visit and enjoy these meadow, wetland and forest habitats in an eco-friendly manner using the more than six kilometres of trails that meander through this restored green space.

Wetland in Bob Hunter Memorial Park Photo: © Gleannan Perrett

Rouge Beach and Marsh in fall

National Urban Park will now be protected providing local fruit and vegetables for the Greater Toronto Area – and beyond.

The history of Rouge National Urban Park is not a long one, but it has been a fairly active one. In 2011 the Government of Canada floated the idea of establishing the country's first national urban park in the GTA. In 2013, the Government of Canada and Province of Ontario agreed to transfer lands to Parks Canada for Rouge National Urban Park.

Canada's first national urban park had a busy year in 2014. The Government of Canada tabled the *Rouge National Urban Park Act* and released the park's draft management plan and embarked on a public consultation program about it. Late in 2014, the cities of Toronto, Markham and Pickering, along with the regional municipalities of York and Durham and the Toronto and Region Conservation Authority, all agreed to transfer lands to Parks Canada for RNUP.

Important steps toward the future of RNUP also occurred in 2015. On January 26, 2015 the House of Commons passed the *Rouge National Urban Park Act*, which received Royal Assent in April. Also that month more than 19 square kilometres of land was transferred to the park from Transport Canada. The park was formally established when the *Rouge National Urban Park Act* came into force on May 15, 2015.

Another significant addition to RNUP

involved the Government of Canada adding an additional 21 square kilometres of land to the park in the City of Pickering and the Township of Uxbridge. And meaningful changes to the park continue. In June 2016, the Government of Canada tabled amendments to the *Rouge National Urban Park Act* that would see the park's ecological integrity be given the first priority in management of RNUP. These amendments also allow longer-term leases for those who farm here.

To help guide the establishment, management and operations of RNUP, Parks Canada established a First Nations Advisory Circle with the First Nations that have a historic connection to the park. Members of this group work with Parks Canada on various initiatives including archaeological fieldwork, visitor experience activities and restoration projects.

HABITATS

Rouge National Urban Park consists of a variety of habitats. Wetlands within RNUP include rivers, streams, marshes, swamps, ponds and the lakeshore where the Rouge River meets Lake Ontario. Meadows, fields, river valleys and forests make up some of the terrestrial habitats while numerous farms also punctuate the park.

A popular wetland habitat in RNUP is Rouge Beach and Marsh. Where the Rouge River meets Lake Ontario is a scenic beach and a large impressive marsh. This is a good spot to observe wildlife.

Urban structures are part of Rouge National Urban Park

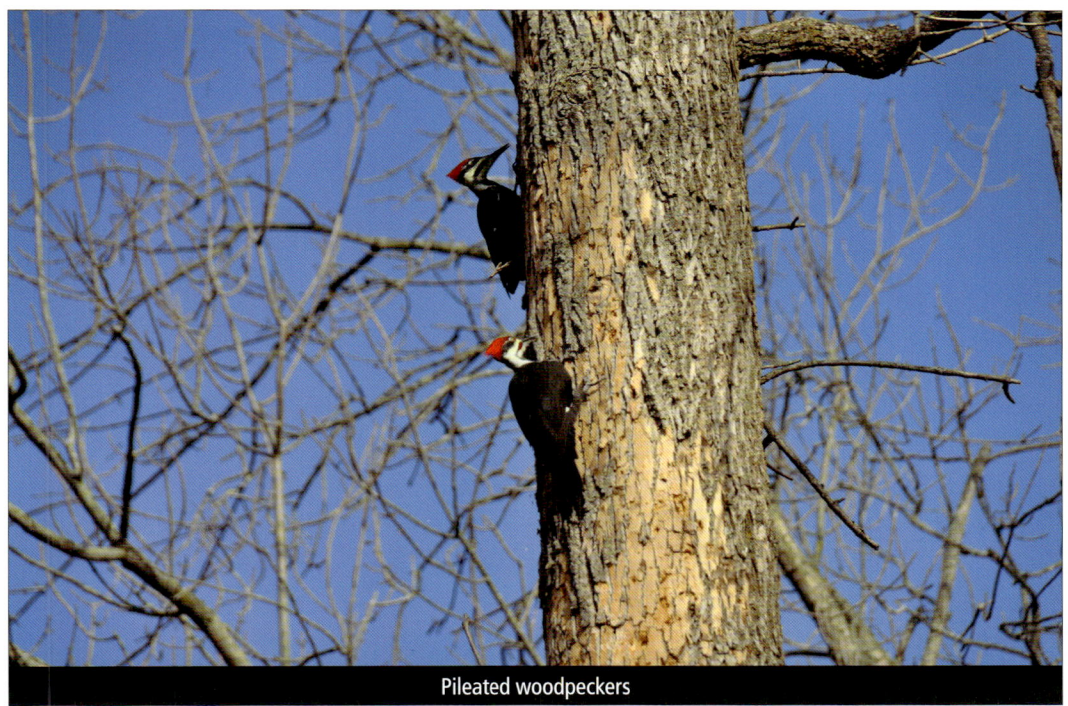
Pileated woodpeckers

The Rouge River itself is an important wetland that flows from the Oak Ridges Moraine to Lake Ontario. Little Rouge Creek (also known as Little Rouge River) is another branch of the Rouge River Watershed. These and the other wetlands within RNUP provide homes for a wide range of species as well as important stopover areas for migrating birds.

Also found within Rouge National Urban Park is important and rare Carolinian habitat. Here you will find southern species of trees such as black walnut, sycamore and burr oak mixing with northern species such as eastern hemlock, white spruce and eastern white pine.

While there is a rich diversity of plant and tree species in RNUP, there is little interior forest habitat left. Farming, urban development and roads transformed once large forests into thin strips of wooded areas or destroyed the forests altogether. The result is that there are few forested areas remaining in and around the park that are large enough to contain quality interior forest habitat.

Collectively, the habitats in RNUP provide a vital ecological corridor allowing plants and animals to live and travel. This eco-corridor links to other wilderness areas along the lake shoreline and to the north that provide more opportunities for species to migrate, thereby decreasing inbreeding and increasing biodiversity.

GEOLOGY

The local bedrock of the Rouge River Watershed is the Whitby Formation which is a shale formation dating back some 450 million years. Most of this bedrock lies beneath sediments that were deposited when the last glacier receded approximately 12,000 years ago. While most of the bedrock is covered by sediment, there are areas, including along the banks of the Rouge River and Little Rouge Creek, where outcrops can be seen.

As the glacier melted and receded it formed Lake Iroquois which covered the area. The shoreline of this ancient lake went through what is now the Beare Road Landfill although most of the old shoreline has been removed for its aggregates.

In their book *Toronto Rocks: The Geological Legacy of the Toronto Region,* Nick Eyles and Laura Clinton describe what often became of abandoned quarries in the area.

"Abandoned pits and quarries along the gravelly beach of Glacial Lake Iroquois and the Niagara Escarpment, were prime sites for 'reclamation' by being infilled with industrial and residential waste...Beare Road Landfill illustrates the fate of many abandoned gravel pits along the Iroquois shoreline. This site received 10 million tonnes of waste, including 180 million litres of liquid waste, from 1969 to 1985."

In some areas of the park, erosion by the Rouge River has created magnificent bluffs including those at the Finch Meander and in

A mink near the mouth of the Rouge River

Fall colours in Rouge National Urban Park

the Twyn Rivers Drive area. The force of the river has created steep riverside bluffs that expose the various layers of glacial deposits. Due to its importance, the Finch Meander has been designated an Area of Natural and Scientific Interest (ANSI).

Other glacial features found in RNUP include drumlins and glacial erratics.

FLORA & FAUNA

More than 1,700 species live in RNUP. There are indeed a number of factors contributing to such rich biodiversity. Certainly the park's size contributes to the numerous plants and animals that live here. Extending from Toronto at Lake Ontario in the south into the Township of Uxbridge in the north and featuring a variety of aquatic and terrestrial habitats, RNUP accommodates a good diversity of plants, birds, mammals, fishes, reptiles, amphibians and invertebrates.

Besides its size, location and variety of habitats, the park's moderate climate contributes to the rich biodiversity found within the park. Parts of the Rouge Valley near Lake Ontario experience a relatively warm climate due largely to the moderating effects of the lake. It is also situated between two forest types – mixed forest as well as Carolinian forest – another contributing factor.

The southern part of the Rouge River Watershed features some Carolinian forest to

PARTICIPATING AT RNUP

The Rouge offers people various ways to get involved with the park. Volunteers can participate in a variety of activities that entail gathering information about animals in the park. Participants not only help collect valuable information, but they have fun meeting others, learning about nature while enjoying an outdoor experience in a natural setting.

Programs and events with RNUP involve a variety of monitoring and educational activities including a Winter Bird Count and the collection of data on the status of various other animals including frogs, salamanders and bees. Other activities include building, installing and monitoring bird houses, planting native trees and wildflowers and picking up garbage.

Two popular volunteer activities are the "Hoot & Howl" and "Frog Watch "described on page 156. Whether you hear an owl or a coyote, the evening is always a success as participants learn more about these animals and enjoy a short hike on a winter's night. The Frog Watch occurs in the park each spring. As opposed to the Hoot & Howl which involves a commitment of only one evening, participants in Frog Watch need to set aside an evening each month from April to June.

Rouge offers a variety of enjoyable ways to experience and contribute to the park so consider participating – and have fun!

Green frog

Mute swan

Kayaking the Rouge River

go along with the other, largely mixed forests, found elsewhere in the park. Rare in Canada, this Carolinian forest makes a significant contribution to the park's diversity because it extends into a transition zone where many southern species reach their northern limits.

While there is not much Carolinian forest habitat in Canada, what is here features an incredible diversity of plant species. The remaining Carolinian forest exists in heavily populated areas of Canada where the vast majority of land is privately owned. Maintaining the Carolinian forest habitat left in Southern Ontario involves both preserving existing Carolinian forest and ensuring responsible stewardship of it on privately-owned lands. The creation of RNUP ensures that the Carolinian forest within the park's boundaries will be protected.

Rouge National Urban Park is home to more than 760 plant species including many species at risk. Several species of trees associated with Carolinian forests are found in the park including: blue-beech, eastern hop-hornbeam, honeylocust, staghorn sumac, nannyberry, white oak, burr oak, red oak, witch-hazel, American beech, shagbark hickory, black walnut, basswood, white ash, black ash, red ash, sycamore, hawthorns, prickly-ash, sugar maple, red maple, silver maple, black maple, choke cherry, black cherry.

Some of the vegetation communities

Woodland Trail

in the park include lakeshore marshes, riverside meadows as well as mixed forests and forests of oak, pine and maple. The rich plant life in RNUP include various species of violet, buttercup, sedge, fern, scouring-rush and goldenrod. Several kinds of strawberry, raspberry, milkweed and duckweed also reside in the park. Two types of lady's slipper, water-lily along with both red trillium and white trillium are in RNUP. There is also Canada wild ginger, wild basil, American ginseng and hundreds of other species – including many that are at risk.

While plant species are well represented in this urban park, so too are the birds. More than 225 species of birds, including more than 120 species that breed in the park, have been recorded here. Rouge National Urban Park is also an important stopover area for migrating birds. The urban park is also home to many at-risk species of birds.

Birds recorded in the park include nine species of gulls, three species of swans, close to 30 species of warblers along with numerous species of hawks, owls, ducks and woodpeckers. Some other species that have visited RNUP include: chimney swift, common nighthawk, yellow-billed cuckoo, black-billed cuckoo, trumpeter swan, bobolink, bald eagle, barn swallow, least bittern, osprey, king rail, eastern bluebird, eastern meadowlark, great egret and green heron.

There are approximately 40 mammal species in RNUP including seven species of bats, five species of mice along with two species of mole, two shrew species and the meadow vole. Three species of squirrels – eastern grey squirrel, red squirrel, northern flying squirrel – along with the eastern chipmunk can also be found in the park. Members of the weasel family have been observed in RNUP including the short-tailed weasel, long-tailed weasel, mink and fisher. Other park residents include: beavers, muskrats, river otters, coyotes, snowshoe hares, white-tailed deer, red foxes, woodchucks, Virginia opossums, porcupines, striped skunks, raccoons, eastern cottontails and black bears.

More than 20 species of reptiles and amphibians have been recorded as well, including eight species of frogs along with the

American toad. Three species of salamanders also live here along with the eastern newt and the mudpuppy. There are also seven species of snakes in RNUP including the at-risk milksnake. The park is also home to four species of at-risk turtles: Blanding's, northern map, snapping and painted. Efforts have been made to ensure that turtles remain an important part of the park and actions to help achieve this goal have included releasing young Blanding's turtles into park wetlands.

The waters of RNUP feature more than 60 fish species including some species at risk. Eight species of shiner are found here along with four species of darter, five kinds of dace and species of perch and minnows. Three kinds of bass – rock, largemouth, smallmouth – are also in the park along with two species of crappie – black crappie and white crappie. Other fish species that have been recorded in RNUP include: American eel, bowfin, pumpkinseed, sea lamprey, white sucker and brown bullhead.

As you might expect there is a rich diversity of invertebrates as well, including a lengthy list of more than 140 butterflies and moths.

More than 60 species of odonates, including some at-risk species, are also park residents. Dragonflies and damselflies are odonates in the Order Odonata, which means "toothed." Odonates have lived on this planet for 300 million years or more. Dragonflies are stronger fliers than damselflies and can take off vertically, fly backwards, hover and attain speeds in excess of 50 kilometres per hour.

Bob Hunter Memorial Park

ACTIVITIES

Visitors to Rouge National Urban Park can enjoy a variety of activities from hiking, camping and picnicking to photography, nature appreciation and bird watching. Water activities include swimming, canoeing and kayaking while in winter some areas are good for hiking, snowshoeing and cross-country skiing.

Hiking is a popular activity in RNUP and there are many trails available. Beginning in the south there is the Rouge Beach Trail. This one-kilometre-long trail provides a stunning view of Lake Ontario as well as the expansive marshes and Rouge Beach.

A little northwest of Rouge Beach is the Mast Trail which you can access from Glen Rouge Campground. Mast Trail is part of an old logging route and is a little over two kilometres long. This footpath extends from near the Glen Rouge Campground to the Twyn Rivers Area and features mature forest.

A little northwest of the Mast Trail is the Glen Eagles Vista Trail. Although only approximately half a kilometre in length, this trail offers very good views of the Rouge River and the Little Rouge Creek valleys as well as a Carolinian forest.

At the Twyn Rivers Area, located east of the Glen Eagles Vista Trail, hikers can access two more trails – the two-kilometre Orchard Trail and the 1.6-kilometre Vista Trail. The Orchard Trail includes regenerating forests while the Vista Trail offers views of bluffs, river

Wetlands are vital for birds like these mallards

Paddling the Rouge River

valleys, forest and meadows.

Across from the Twyn Rivers Area is the Celebration Forest. This park memorial honours friends and supporters of the park and has a short, half-kilometre trail.

At the north end of Orchard Trail is the Beare Loop Trailhead where you can access the Cedar Trail and where you can see the old landfill-site hill. Cedar Trail is a little over two kilometres long and follows Little Rouge Creek. Walking this scenic trail you will see mature forest, meadows and wetlands.

Located west of Cedar Trail is the Finch Meander Area where you can hike the 250-metre-long Finch Meander Trail. This scenic Trail contains old maple trees and follows a curve of the Rouge River.

Continuing north past Cedar Trail you come to the Woodland Trail and the Woodlands Area. Woodland Trail is 2.7-kilometres long that is a fairly easy walk for approximately half of the footpath and then turns into a moderately challenging hike. This trail features forest, meadows and Little Rouge Creek.

A little farther north, more trails await in the Bob Hunter Memorial Park which is located north of Steeles Avenue in Markham. Part of Rouge National Urban Park, this park celebrates the life of Robert Hunter who was an environmentalist, journalist and one of the founders of Greenpeace. The footpaths here take you through, or near, meadows, wetlands

Rouge River near Lake Ontario

and forests.

For those who like to camp, there is the Glen Rouge Campground located in Toronto. Situated along the banks of the Rouge River, this campground has more than a hundred campsites on 8.7 hectares of land offering a camping experience to those who live in the Greater Toronto Area.

Those interested in seeing some of the park from the water can canoe or kayak the Rouge River. A good place to start is at the Rouge Beach and Marsh and paddle north. The marsh in this area is a fascinating place and fun to explore by canoe or kayak.

Beachgoers and those wanting to go swimming can enjoy these activities at the Rouge Beach.

There are also some picnic facilities located within RNUP. The park's varied habitats, beautiful scenery and rich diversity of flora and fauna provide good opportunities for bird watching, photography and nature appreciation. Cycling is also allowed in some areas, although not on the trails (except on the Waterfront Trail). There are also educational programs and activities available in RNUP throughout the year.

Visitors to the park in winter will find invigorating things to do. Hiking the trails provides good exercise and an opportunity to see some of the animals out and about in the park during the winter months. Snowshoeing and cross-country skiing are other winter activities you can enjoy in RNUP although trails are not maintained in winter and conditions are not always suitable for these activities. Remember to stay on the trails.

There are some winter park programs and activities you can get involved with such as the popular Winter Bird Count where you identify and record birds that provide scientists with valuable information. There is also a program where you can learn more about coyotes and owls in RNUP.

For more information: www.parkscanada.gc.ca/rouge

OUR PARK ADVENTURES

In mid October, Lynn and I experienced fall's beautiful colours in several areas of RNUP including the Glen Rouge Campground,

Beare Hill and the Rouge Beach and Marsh where the sight of the GO Train reminds us that our "wilderness excursion" was actually occurring in an urban area. We have also enjoyed a fall hike on the Woodland Trail that included scenic meadows, forest and Little Rouge Creek.

****

Lynn and I arrived at Rouge Beach and Marsh in late October. It was a bright, chilly morning and we were about to canoe the Rouge River courtesy of Parks Canada. We began our trip at Rouge Beach and paddled the Rouge River up to Highway 401 and then back – a return trip of approximately 4.5 kilometres. You can paddle under and past the 401 but will need to negotiate a series of portages soon after. The river here is relatively shallow with a sandy bottom and sandbanks forming along long stretches and at sharp curves. At the beginning of our canoe trip we saw a mink watching us from some rocks on shore. I have to admit that I was somewhat surprised seeing a mink in the urban park – and so soon into our trip. But I soon learned that while mink are not abundant in this area, they are not as uncommon as you might think.

The paddle offered scenic views of the river along with marshes and forests that still possessed some of their fine fall colours. Birds were abundant. At one bend in the river we came across numerous mallards. A little farther upstream we saw two pileated

Glen Rouge Campground

woodpeckers high up in a tree. They were later joined by a smaller woodpecker, either a downy woodpecker or a hairy.

As we continued up river we occasionally got stuck as the water levels were quite low. By seeking out deeper areas of river, we were able to make our way up to Highway 401. The scenery was beautiful — and we easily forgot we were near the busiest highway in the world!

The return downstream was likewise enjoyable so we finished out the trip canoeing around the marsh near the mouth of the Rouge. With the exception of some kayakers, we didn't encounter anyone else on the river!

****

In late February we attended the Hoot & Howl event in Bob Hunter Memorial Park located in the northern part of RNUP. The fun and informative evening included a presentation on owls and coyotes as well as a short hike where we attempted to communicate with the local owl and coyote population.

There were a little more than 20 people in our group. As we walked the trail we would occasionally stop and remain quiet. Our leader would then play some recorded owl calls in the hopes of getting a response. This event is held at this time of year as owls, who are territorial, are mating and communicating by sound. Large owls often attack smaller ones, so the group leader started off calling the smallest owls first. If the call wasn't successful then a call for the next largest owl species was played.

Wetland in Beare Hill area

One of many scenic wetlands found within Rouge National Urban Park

The four owls called were: northern saw-whet owl, eastern screech owl, barred owl and great horned owl. The calls on this night were unfortunately unsuccessful.

We also attempted to communicate with some resident coyotes. Our group called out in unison "yip-yip-yahoo." While I didn't hear any responses, some members said they heard a distant coyote call back.

Coyotes are intelligent and incredible animals. Unfortunately, they are also despised and feared by many. Events such as the Hoot & Howl help educate our species about the important roles that these fascinating animals play in nature and how we can peacefully co-exist with them.

Since this event can be taxing for the animals, particularly owls who are territorial and would be stressed by new owls called into their area, it is held only once a year. Taking a short walk on a winter's night, listening for coyotes and owls and meeting other people interested in these activities is a good way to get out and enjoy nature. While our calls weren't successful, we learned quite a bit about these creatures and enjoyed a fun night in the park.

****

We returned to Rouge National Urban Park in spring. Accompanying us was our daughter Gleannan and this time we were taking part in the Frog Watch program. This monitoring program included an education and training workshop as well as three evening outings over spring (April, May and June) to gather information about frogs in RNUP. Participants at the workshop were divided into groups. Each group was assigned a different location to monitor. Our group would monitor frogs in three wetlands in Bob Hunter Memorial Park.

Our group's first Frog Watch occurred late in April when we visited our wetlands at dusk. The temperature was around 5°C. While we didn't hear any frogs this night, it was still a good experience. We even saw a muskrat, a family of geese – and a shooting star! The second and third Frog Watch evenings took place near the end of May and the end of June. Here we heard a multiplicity of frogs including gray treefrogs and green frogs. We also saw red-winged blackbirds and mallards, among others.

Walking trails and monitoring several wetlands for frogs, and other animals, was a memorable way to spend an evening. Lynn, Gleannan and I had fun enjoying each other's company in these scenic settings. We also got to meet others who had similar interests in nature, animals and RNUP. Frog Watch is an important monitoring program that helps assess the health of the urban park's wetlands. Frogs are an indicator species and wetlands, with a good population of frogs and various frog species, do tell us about the health of these ecosystems.

Darkness descends on a wetland Photo: © Gleannan Perrett

The GO Train at Rouge Beach and Marsh

ROUGE NATIONAL URBAN PARK

The view of Landon Bay from a lookout

7. THOUSAND ISLANDS NATIONAL PARK

"We must begin thinking like a river if we are to leave a legacy of beauty and life for future generations." – David Brower

Thousand Islands National Park (TINP) is one of Canada's oldest — and smallest — national parks. Formerly known as St. Lawrence Islands National Park, TINP was established in 1904 and covers approximately 24 square kilometres. According to Parks Canada's 2010 management plans, "the park consists of all or part of 26 islands and 80 islets and shoals located along a 100-kilometre stretch of the St. Lawrence River, as well as a series of mainland properties." Mainland properties with facilities are at Mallorytown Landing, Landon Bay and Jones Creek. Other mainland park properties include the Skoryna Nature Reserve. Two islands at the east end of Lake Ontario, Main Duck Island and Yorkshire Island, are also managed by the park for a possible future national marine conservation area.

Surrounding TINP is the Frontenac Arch Biosphere Reserve (FABR), as designated in 2002 by

> **THOUSAND ISLANDS NATIONAL PARK**
> - Consists of numerous islands, islets and shoals along the St. Lawrence River
> - Canada's fifth oldest national park
> - Located where the Frontenac Arch meets the St. Lawrence River
> - Bird migration corridor
> - Excellent island camping opportunities

Thousand Islands National Park
Ontario, Canada
Brockville
Gananoque
Kingston
401
15
United States of America
Thousand Islands National Park Boundary
Lake Ontario
Map: © Parks Canada
Contains information licensed under the Open Government Licence – Ontario
The Government of Canada, Parks Canada Agency cannot be held accountable for errors or omissions in the information displayed on this map.
©2017 . Her Majesty the Queen in Right of Canada
0 5 10
Kilometers

Thousand Islands National Park Jones Creek
Highway 401
International Border
St. Lawrence River
Jones Creek Trail System
Boucle Bear Loop
Boucle Eel Loop
Boucle Hawk Loop
Boucle Heron Loop
Boucle Snipe Loop
Boucle Turtle Loop
Bridge - Pont
Sentier Access Trail
Sentier Deer Trail
Sentier Wolf Trail
Thousand Islands National Park Boundary
Map: © Parks Canada
Contains information licensed under the Open Government Licence – Ontario
The Government of Canada, Parks Canada Agency cannot be held accountable for errors or omissions in the information displayed on this map.
©2017 . Her Majesty the Queen in Right of Canada
0 500 1,000
Meters

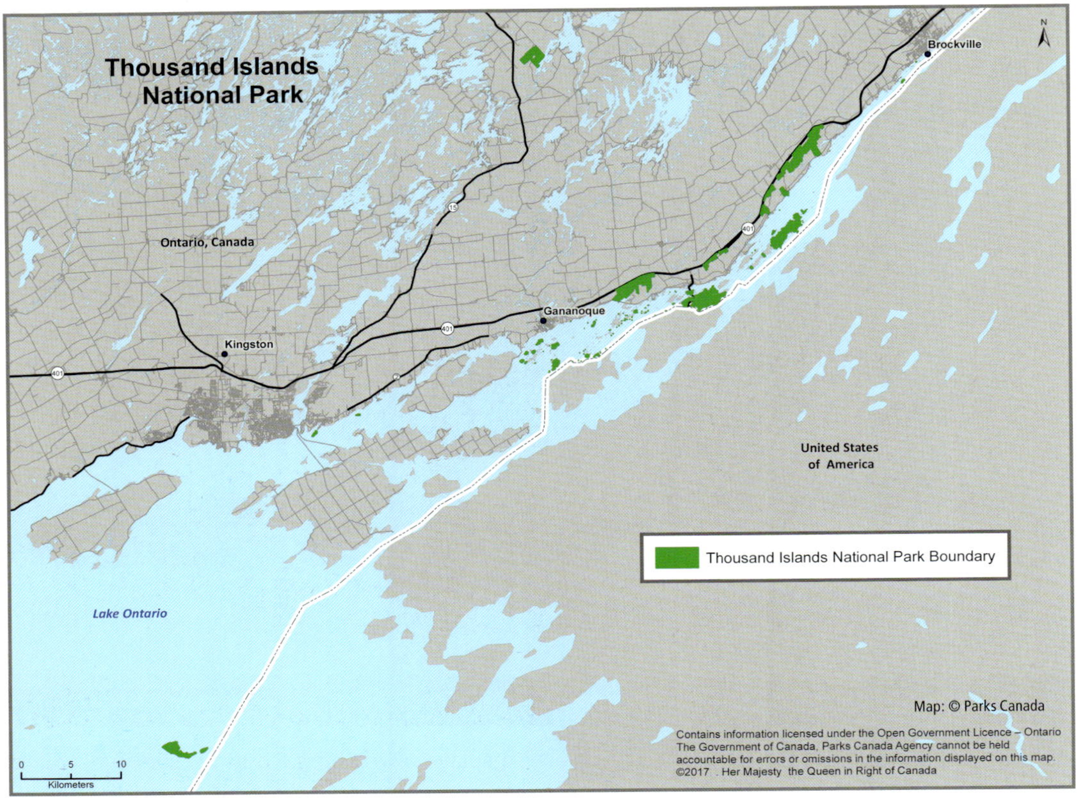

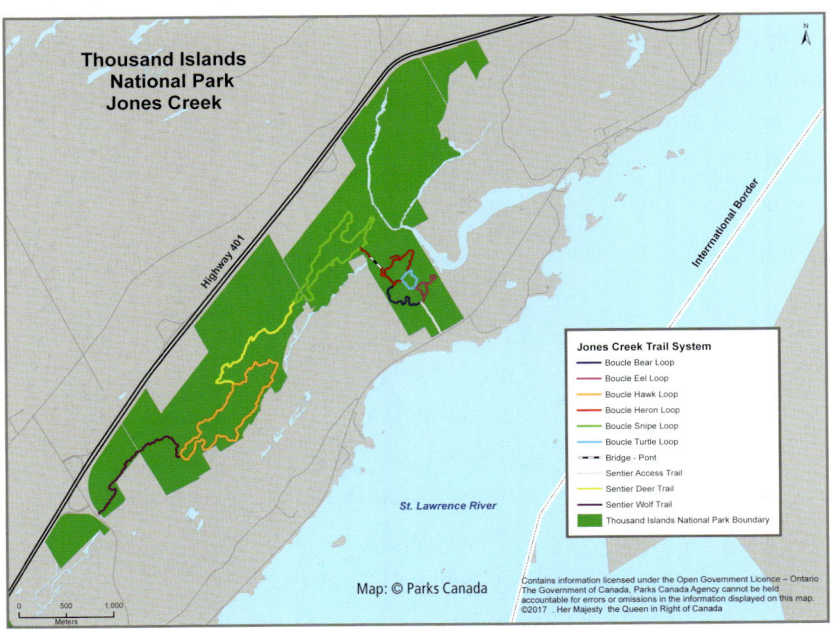

This gazebo on Gordon Island was built between 1904 and 1907

the United Nations Educational, Scientific, and Cultural Organization (UNESCO). The "Biosphere Reserve" designation is given to internationally significant ecosystems and promotes their protection and sustainable use. Thousand Islands National Park is protected while offering sustainable activities for visitors to enjoy and get a better appreciation of this special place.

Thousand Islands National Park's mainland properties offer a variety of activities including hiking and picnicking. The islands are accessible by boat where campsites and trails await. Other services available elsewhere in the park include docking, picnic facilities, swimming, drinking water, interpretive displays, barbecues, vehicle parking and a boat launch area. If you don't have your own boat you can rent one or use a water taxi from one of the marinas or outfitters. You can also enjoy the beauty of the Thousand Islands from a tour boat that travels the St. Lawrence River amongst the scenic islands.

PARK HISTORY

Thousand Islands National Park is Canada's fifth oldest national park and the first established east of the Rocky Mountains. Created in 1904, the park features more than 25 islands, approximately 80 islets and shoals in the St. Lawrence River stretching between Kingston and Brockville. (Jacques

Drystone Archway at Landon Bay leads into a beautiful deciduous forest

Cartier named the river after first sailing it in 1535.) The park also manages Main Duck Island and Yorkshire Island at the east end of Lake Ontario. Located along the boundary between Ontario and New York State, TINP is situated in one of North America's most popular summer vacation spots.

The area in and around Thousand Islands has an interesting human history that included settlement as far back as 9000 years ago – and possibly even longer. This occupation is described in the book *St. Lawrence Islands National Park* by Don Ross.

"Nomadic hunters and explorers by nature, the first people came to the Thousand Islands perhaps about 7000 BC. Very little is known of their material possessions; nothing is known of their lifestyle and language. The people and their era are called 'Plano Culture.'"

Ross goes on to mention that a piece of a stone hunting point, which was "typically the work of Plano Culture people," was discovered at a Gordon Island campsite.

First Nations peoples continued to live in the area that they called "Garden of the Great Spirit," the traditional name for Thousand Islands. Europeans arrived in the seventeenth century and they used the river as a trade route. The first Europeans to settle in here were the United Empire Loyalists from the United States

Words of the Haudenosaunee Thanksgiving Address at Contemplation Rock at Mallorytown Landing Photo: © Parks Canada

A Mohawk rock carving at Mallorytown Landing

who came here in the late 1700s.

The sixteenth century also saw the Battle of the Thousand Islands from August 16 – 24, 1760. The naval battle involved primarily British and French forces and took place as the Seven Years' War was nearing an end.

Thousand Islands, of which there are more than 1800 with the majority located on the Canadian side of the border, were not explored, surveyed or named until around the War of 1812. The islands on the Canadian side were named and charted by Captain William Fitzwilliam Owen who was with the Royal Navy. Many of the island group names are associated with the military and include the Admiralty Islands, the Navy Islands and the Lake Fleet Islands. The individual Admiralty islands were named after British Lords of the Admiralty while the Navy islands were named after officers in the Royal Navy. The names in the Lake Fleet islands came from ships in the Royal Navy. The easternmost group are the Brock Islands named after Sir Isaac Brock, a Major-General with the British Army who died in the War of 1812.

Four decades after the War of 1812 ended, control of islands on the Canadian side was retained by the Indian Branch of the Department of the Interior as described in the book, *Life on the Edge: The Cultural Landscape of the Thousand Islands Area*.

"While the state gradually incorporated First Nation's lands throughout the Frontenac Axis into the national demesne, the Mississaugas retained title to the islands in the St. Lawrence as far as Prescott. There they had lived during the fishing-season, foraying out along the Frontenac Axis during hunting season. Even after their several cessions of lands throughout the backcountry, they continued to lay claim to the islands in the St. Lawrence, leasing some to local residents. In June 1856, this last vestige of the Mississauga formal presence came to an end with Surrender No. 77 by which they relinquished their control of the islands to the Indian Branch of the Department of the Interior in return for certain benefits."

While Thousand Islands National Park wasn't established until 1904, the idea of setting aside some islands that the public could use was raised as early as the 1870s. In 1874, the islands acquired from the Mississaugas were made a "Dominion Park." In 1904 the following islands became the first islands of this national park: Aubrey, Mermaid, Beau Rivage, Camelot, Endymion, Gordon, Georgina, Constance and Adelaide. These range in size from as small as a hectare and a half in the case of Mermaid to almost 10 hectares for both Camelot and Georgina. Stovin Island and part of Grenadier Island soon came under the park umbrella.

Another acquisition to TINP in 1904 was the Mallorytown Landing property donated by the Mallory family. In 1959 a larger addition to

St Lawrence River near Hill Island

this property was donated. Since establishment of the park many other islands have also been added. In most cases Parks Canada owns the entire island, while in cases such as Grenadier Island, Hill Island, McDonald Island and Hay Island, only parts of these islands are park property.

The Thousand Islands International Bridge officially opened in 1938. It was built largely to accommodate the increased use of automobiles and the spiking popularity of the area in general. Thousand Islands International Bridge links Ontario to New York State and spans both Constance Island and Georgina Island in the park. It also provides access to Hill Island.

Complementing the Mallorytown Landing property are the mainland properties at Jones Creek and Landon Bay. Located between Highway 401 and the 1000 Islands Parkway, Jones Creek offers numerous trails ranging from short walks under a kilometre to longer hikes around four kilometres in length.

Located on the 1000 Islands Parkway between Gananoque and Ivy Lea is the Landon Bay property. This part of the park boasts various scenic hiking trails and a fine scenic lookout.

The Thousand Islands area has experienced a long rich history. Today, it is one of North America's most storied and popular vacation retreat and tourist destinations where summer homes, cottages and other recreational developments abound. Thousand Islands National Park is an important part of this.

Thousand Islands International Bridge

ST. LAWRENCE RIVER

The more than 1,800 islands that make up the Thousand Islands sit smack dab in the historic St. Lawrence River. The Gulf of St. Lawrence and subsequently, the St. Lawrence River, were named by French explorer Jacques Cartier who arrived in the Gulf off Anticosti Island on August 10, 1535. That day marked the Feast of Saint Lawrence, who was martyred in 258 CE.

Flowing east from Lake Ontario to the Gulf of the St. Lawrence, the St. Lawrence River is just under 1,200 kilometres long. The St. Lawrence hydrographic system, which includes the Great Lakes, is more than 3,000 kilometres in length extending into Minnesota. This system is one of the largest in the world and the third largest in North America, after the Mississippi River and the Mackenzie River. It drains approximately 1.6 million square kilometres of watershed.

Formed after the last glacier receded, the St. Lawrence River has played a significant role in Canada's history. It formed an ancient transportation route important to First Nations, then to the fur trade and the subsequent exploration of much of North America, and then the timber industries. The 1959 creation of the St. Lawrence Seaway, opening a safe shipping route from the Great Lakes through to the Atlantic Ocean, continues the river's importance to modern transport and commerce.

St. Lawrence River at Mallorytown Landing

HABITATS

Although Thousand Islands National Park is small for a national park, it features a good diversity of habitats. The park is located where two biogeographic features meet – the Frontenac Arch and the St. Lawrence River. The Frontenac Arch is an extension of the Canadian Shield that connects Algonquin Provincial Park to the Adirondack Mountains in New York State; while the St. Lawrence River connects the Great Lakes to the Atlantic Ocean. As a result, the area in and around the park contains a variety of terrestrial and aquatic habitats.

Forest habitat is prominently featured throughout the park both on the mainland

Oak tree on Gordon Island

properties and islands. While the park has some old growth forests, other secondary forests have grown from abandoned agricultural fields. Future forests in the park are promoted through use of plantings and prescribed fires.

Wetlands are also well represented here. Jones Creek, a tributary of the St. Lawrence River, features various wetlands to go along with its rocky ridges and forests of oak, beech, maple, hemlock, pine and birch. These wetlands include streams, creeks, and a marsh. Wetlands are also featured at Mallorytown Landing as is woodland habitat. Another of the park's mainland properties, Skoryna Nature Reserve, also has important wetlands.

The many types of habitats result in a myriad of animals and plants. Along with the park's forest and wetland habitats, plants and animals are also abundant in the park's other habitats that include rocky areas, cliffs, shorelines and fields.

Much of the park consists of islands spread out over a considerable length of the St. Lawrence River. And each island is unique. Hill Island, for instance, sports a mix of vibrant forests punctuated by fields, ravines and marshes. Similarly, Grenadier Island, on which the park has several properties, has everything from swamp woods, old fields, oak forests and expansive, lush marsh as well as rocky shorelines.

Other park islands also feature a variety of important habitat. Camelot Island is rocky with steep cliffs and features a forested interior while Gordon Island is a sandstone-based island with deep soils. McDonald Island was used for farming and now features regenerating forests and fields.

GEOLOGY

The stunning landscapes of the Thousand Islands aren't new. In fact, they have been more than a billion years in the making and began when sediments were deposited on the floor of an ancient sea. The massive weight of the vast layers of sediment – combined with pressure and heat – turned these sediments into sedimentary rock such as limestone, sandstone and shale. Molten rock deep in the earth forced its way up through fractures sending towering mountains skyward. More heat and pressure along with molten rock formed metamorphic and igneous rock at the mountain roots. These ancient rocks eventually eroded to a relatively flat surface. Fast forward to approximately 600 million years ago — here the land was again flooded and more sediments settled to the seafloor where they accumulated on the pre-existing ancient mountain roots. In his book *St. Lawrence Islands National Park*, Don Ross describes what happened next.

Limberlost on Hill Island is used by the Canadian Coast Guard

"About the same time that the sandstone-creating seas lay upon the land, a slow uplift of the old mountain roots took place. A gentle arch – the Frontenac Arch – was formed, its axis running southeast from the Madawaska region to the Adirondack Mountains. Although the uplift halted hundreds of millions of years ago, the granite of the Frontenac Arch remains as the backbone of south-central Canada and divides the otherwise level plains of southern Ontario."

Fast forward again to approximately three million years ago when glaciers covered much of North America. These glaciers extended across most of Canada during at least four separate stages. The last ice age ended approximately 10,000 years ago and this glacier, which was two to three kilometres thick, advanced across the Thousand Islands region and into the northern United States. As the climate warmed, the glacier retreated north and northeast across Ontario leaving large quantities of rock, gravel, mud and other material that created hills and filled valleys. Meltwaters created landforms including a large esker – a sand and gravel ridge – that runs the length of Grenadier Island.

The ice also carved out the basins that would become the Great Lakes. The incredible weight of the glaciers also depressed the land by hundreds of metres to the point where the St. Lawrence and Ottawa River valleys were below sea level. As the last glacier retreated and no longer blocked the Atlantic Ocean, water flowed up the St. Lawrence valley into eastern Ontario as far as what is now Brockville, as well as into southern Quebec, thereby creating the Champlain Sea. Without the weight of the ice, the land slowly started to rebound and rise again forcing the retreat of the Champlain Sea.

The Thousand Islands area was created when water from the basins for the Great Lakes overflowed on its journey to the sea amongst the rocks of the prehistoric mountains that once dominated this region. The hilltops we see today are what remain of this ancient mountain chain – the Frontenac Arch – and what are now known as the Thousand Islands.

FLORA & FAUNA

The Thousand Islands region has one of the richest diversities of plant and animal species in the country due to the area's numerous forest types, geology, moderate climate, myriad habitats, location and migration corridors.

Situated at the convergence point of the Frontenac Arch and the St. Lawrence River Valley, TINP is where forest regions merge. Included here are the boreal forest of the Canadian Shield; forests of the Adirondack and Appalachian Mountains; and forests of the Atlantic Coast and the Great Lakes. The result is an incredible diversity of flora and fauna along these natural east-west and north-south migration routes.

The Frontenac Arch and its islands also contribute to the region's biodiversity. The islands act as stepping stones assisting birds, mammals and other species to migrate more easily across the St. Lawrence River.

Complementing all this is the area's

Grenadier Island

172 SOUTHERN ONTARIO'S NATIONAL PARKS

FRONTENAC ARCH & THE FRONTENAC ARCH BIOSPHERE RESERVE

The Frontenac Arch, also known as the Frontenac Axis, is an extension of the Canadian Shield that began approximately a billion years ago as a range of mountains. Over hundreds of millions of years these ancient granite mountains have weathered down to their roots, which is what we see today. These "roots" in the St. Lawrence River are now known as the Thousand Islands.

The Frontenac Arch links the boreal forests of the Canadian Shield in Ontario to the forests of the Adirondack and Appalachian Mountains in New York State. First Nations peoples refer to the ancient granite "bridge" as "The Bones of the Mother."

Where the Frontenac Arch meets the St. Lawrence River is a crossroads where five forest regions come together resulting in an incredible

Landon Bay area

diversity of plants and animals. These north-south, east-west corridors along with a moderate climate allow some species to extend their furthermost ranges into this area. The Frontenac Arch is home to many of Ontario's species at risk.

The importance of this special place was recognized in 2002 by UNESCO which designated the Frontenac Arch a biosphere reserve. Biosphere reserves are globally important ecosystems that are protected while encouraging sustainable development. Helping to organize and manage programs within the Frontenac Arch Biosphere Reserve (FABR) is the non-profit organization Frontenac Arch Biosphere Network (FABN) which is involved in various sustainable activities including education, conservation, hiking and tourism.

For more information:
Frontenac Arch Biosphere Network   www.frontenacarchbiosphere.ca

Mulcaster Island

Spotted joe pye weed

moderate climate which is moderated largely by the Great Lakes to the west. This moderating effect reduces the chances of a deep freeze in winter as well as extremely hot summers. This allows many plant and animal species to reach the limits of their ranges.

Both the short-tailed weasel, found more often in the north, and the long-tailed weasel, found more often in the south, are present here. Similarly, the Frontenac Arch is home to both the northern flying squirrel and the southern flying squirrel. The snowshoe hare, typically found in the north, resides in this area along with the eastern cottontail, a southern species. Northern species such as the fisher, American marten and the lynx also reach their southern limits in the Frontenac Arch. Other mammals who reside in the park include deer, coyotes, foxes, beavers, porcupines, mink, skunks, raccoons and bats.

Wetlands provide homes for the many reptiles and amphibians who live here, including at-risk species such as the eastern musk turtle, northern map turtle, snapping turtle, Blanding's turtle, five-lined skink (Ontario's only lizard), gray ratsnake, eastern ribbonsnake and milksnake. Amphibians, including frogs and salamanders, are well represented in the park with the western chorus frog being an at-risk species. In his book *St. Lawrence Islands National Park*, Don Ross says that Hill Island has all nine species of snakes as well as many of the frog species found in the area.

There are various reasons why a species becomes an "at-risk" species. In the St. Lawrence River and its environs the Blanding's turtle is impacted not only by habitat loss and degradation – a common threat to many species – but also by nest predation and collection for the pet trade.

The Frontenac Arch is a vital bird migration corridor and provides important habitat for birds breeding and nesting here. Well in excess of a hundred species of birds have been recorded in this area including at-risk species such as: least bittern, eastern whip-poor-will, golden-winged warbler, cerulean warbler, Canada warbler, common nighthawk, peregrine falcon, rusty blackbird, barn swallow, bobolink, eastern meadowlark, eastern wood-pewee, wood thrush, Louisiana waterthrush, eastern loggerhead shrike, Henslow's sparrow, northern bobwhite, red headed woodpecker, short-eared owl, yellow rail and king rail.

An insect species at risk in the park is the monarch butterfly.

There are approximately 100 species of fish in the St. Lawrence River and the vast majority can be found in the Thousand Islands area. Some fish species at risk include pugnose shiner, grass pickerel, American eel, bridle shiner and the lake sturgeon.

There are approximately 1,000 plant species in TINP with as many as 40 or more considered rare species. There are plant species present from northern boreal forests, southern deciduous forests as well as forests from the east and west. Species from the Atlantic coast such as red spruce and wire birch (also known as grey birch) are at the western limits of their range here.

Plants commonly found in regions to the south also extend to their northern limits in and around the park. Deerberry is one such plant. This at-risk species is known to grow in only four locations in Canada including two islands in TINP. In fact, approximately 95% of all deerberry in Canada is found on two park islands with the majority occurring on Grenadier Island. Deerberry is important as a source of food for birds and it contributes to the area's biodiversity. Habitat loss and damage caused by people leaving the trails

Lookout over Landon Bay

THOUSAND ISLANDS INTERNATIONAL BRIDGE

The Thousand Islands International Bridge extends from Ivy Lea near Gananoque, Ontario to Collins Landing near Alexandria Bay, New York. The 13.7-kilometre bridge provides a connection from Highway 401 in Ontario to US Interstate 81. Operation of the Thousand Islands Bridge system is shared between the Federal Bridge Corporation Limited of Canada and the Thousand Islands Bridge Authority.

Construction of the bridge began on April 30, 1937 with ground-breaking ceremonies conducted at Collins Landing, with work beginning on the foundation for both Canadian and American bridges in May. The Canadian span from abutment to abutment is 1,015 metres and includes the 182.9-metre section connecting Hill Island to Constance Island, a 106.1-metre span from Constance Island to Georgina Island, and a 228.6-metre suspension bridge from Georgina Island to the Canadian mainland. The American span extends from the mainland to Wellesley Island and includes a 243.8-metre suspension bridge. From abutment to abutment the American span is 1,371.6 metres.

The Thousand Islands International Bridge was completed at a cost of just over $3 million. On August 18, 1938 Prime Minister Mackenzie King and President Franklin D. Roosevelt opened the bridges during dedication ceremonies that were attended by thousands. Today more than two million vehicles cross the bridge annually.

threaten this plant.

A rare species more common to southern regions is the pitch pine. Most pitch pine found in Canada is located in the Frontenac Arch including several island's in the park. A ridge on Hill Island contains the largest stand of pitch pine in the Thousand Islands area. In fact, TINP is the only national park in Canada that has pitch pine. In order to help pitch pine, which benefits from fire, Parks Canada conducts some prescribed burns to remove competing vegetation and prepare seedbeds. Prescribed burns have occurred on Georgina Island, Camelot Island and at Mallorytown Landing.

Other species of at-risk plants in the park include: butternut, pale-bellied frost lichen, swamp rose-mallow, eastern prairie fringed orchid and broad beech fern.

Tree species located in and around the park that are commonly found in Carolinian forests include bitternut hickory, bur oak, swamp oak and butternut. Some species found in Ontario's deciduous and coniferous forests present in the park include: red pine, white pine, red oak, red maple, sugar maple, hemlock, beech, white spruce, balsam fir, white birch and basswood.

Despite the protection that this park provides, there are also issues that threaten the species that live there.

The Thousand Islands is a popular destination for cottagers and tourists whose impact on species is not often positive.

Approaching the lookout over Landon Bay

Major roadways, industry, development and agriculture also affect the area's flora and fauna. While plant and animal species are protected, the park's islands and mainland properties are relatively few and spread out over a considerable distance. The park, along with other protected areas, are islands within an area that features considerable development. Genetic exchange between these isolated areas, including park and private islands, is minimized or prevented altogether negatively affecting diversity. Increases in tourism and development also impact the area's biodiversity as does habitat loss and fragmentation – particularly along shorelines and wetlands.

Maintaining biodiversity and healthy

Jones Creek

ecosystems will involve the efforts of TINP along with other organizations such as the Frontenac Arch Biosphere Network (FABN) and the Algonquin to Adirondacks Collaborative (A2A). The Algonquin to Adirondacks Collaborative is a network of partner organizations that is working to connect Algonquin Provincial Park in Ontario to Adirondack Park in New York State across the Frontenac Arch. Private landowners and businesses will also have to play important roles in terms of responsible land stewardship and working to ensure that the ecosystem is healthy.

ACTIVITIES

One of the most popular activities here is boating. Boaters can use the boat launch at Mallorytown Landing or any number of marinas along the St. Lawrence River between Brockville and Kingston. It is recommended that you use accurate navigational charts to help ensure that you avoid shoals and hidden rocks – and don't get lost. Boat rentals are also available at various marinas located near the park.

A pleasant way to see the many islands and fascinating sights in the Thousand Islands is to go on a boat cruise. Tour boats offer cruises of various lengths where you can see the natural beauty of the islands along with historic places, impressive homes and interesting landmarks such as the Thousand Islands International Bridge, Boldt Castle and Singer Castle.

If you want to enjoy TINP from a canoe or kayak you have various options. If you aren't a very experienced paddler you can contact a local outfitting company where you can rent a kayak or canoe along with other equipment and also receive some lessons and go on a guided trip.

Experienced paddlers can explore the islands on their own but should be aware of tour boats and other large vessels that share the river. Large powerboats also create large waves and areas of the river can be windy making canoeing and kayaking not only a rewarding experience, but a challenging and potentially dangerous one as well.

If you plan on swimming in the park

make sure you swim in appropriate locations and take all safety precautions. Visitors are responsible for their own safety. Strong river currents and large ships and powerboats are some things to be aware of and avoid. There are two sand beaches in the park and these are located on Thwartway Island and Grenadier Island – Central. The beach on Grenadier Island is a designated swimming area.

There are many good hikes in the park. Mainland properties at Jones Creek, Landon Bay and Mallorytown Landing have trails. Jones Creek has almost 15 kilometres of trails. Many of the footpaths are fairly short, easy walks while some are between a kilometre and a half and four kilometres in length.

Landon Bay also has several kilometres of trails in the easy to medium difficulty range. The trails allow hikers to experience hemlock and deciduous forests, meadows, rocky outcrops and more. The Lookout Trail provides a stunning view of Landon Bay and the St. Lawrence River. Short trails can be found at Mallorytown Landing and on most of the islands. If you enjoy a nice walk in winter you can snowshoe at Jones Creek where a variety of trails offer short, pleasant strolls, as well as longer more invigorating hikes.

The park's mainland properties and islands provide many opportunities for a picnic as well as places to take photographs or just take in the area's sights, flora and fauna.

In contrast to Fathom Five National Marine Park and Georgian Bay Islands National

Adelaide Island

Park where island camping is limited, both reservable and non-reservable campsites are available on many of the islands at TINP. A few offer fairly comprehensive services to campers including garbage collection, considerable dock space and some even allow generators. These include Grenadier Island - Central, Batterman's Point, Beau Rivage, and MacDonald. On the mainland, Mallorytown Landing is a full-service area.

Most islands are set up for those looking for a quiet, peaceful camping experience in a natural, less crowded setting. These islands often include a small number of primitive campsites, composting toilets and when it comes to garbage, you must follow a pack-in and pack-out policy.

Some islands have no camping but include trails and paddle-landing sites, toilets, mooring buoys and picnic shelters. Firewood is available on many of the islands as well but potable water is not. It is important to plan your outing in advance and learn what services and facilities are offered and any applicable fees. Transportation to the islands is by boat and campers and visitors must arrange their own transport.

If the idea of camping appeals to you but you would prefer a little more comfort you can opt for Parks Canada's oTENTik camping. oTENTiks are described as a cross between a rustic cabin and a tent and feature things like a sleeping area, solar-powered lighting, furniture, deck, picnic table, barbecue and

Raspberry and blackberry plants growing after a prescribed burn on Gordon Island.

Islet in the St. Lawrence River

more. There are numerous oTENTiks at Mallorytown Landing as well as on McDonald Island and Gordon Island.

ISLAND CAMPING & VISITS

Islands in Thousand Islands National Park are quite different from one another. There are numerous reasons for this including their location in the river, how they were affected by glaciation and what they were used for in the past. The following are some of the islands that you might want to include in a visit and some of the things that you can see and do there. While these islands offer quality camping experiences, you must arrange for your own transportation to them.

Most, but not all, offer trails, docks, picnic shelters and firewood. There are toilets on the following islands.

Cedar Island

Cedar Island is located just south of Kingston. The approximately nine-hectare island was acquired by the park in 1924. If you enjoy some human history with your camping this island has the Cathcart Redoubt Martello Tower. Located just off the shore from Fort Henry, this is one of four towers built in the 1840s during a dispute between Great Britain and the United States. The tower, a national historic site, was built to protect Kingston's harbour as well as the entrance

Female mallard

to the Rideau Canal. Cedar Island features mixed deciduous forest and has campsites, docks, a paddle-landing site, a picnic shelter and trails.

Milton Island

Acquired in 1966, Milton Island is approximately three hectares in size and located five kilometres east of Kingston. Red oak, white pine and rock (including outcrops of quartzite) make up part of this island. Facilities include docks, a few campsites and a picnic shelter.

Aubrey Island

Approximately six hectares in size, Aubrey Island is one of the original islands when the park was established in 1904. Vegetation here includes red oak, shagbark hickory, sugar maple as well as a rare sedge. A lighthouse once stood on the island's south bluff and remains of the lighthouse are still evident. There are also campsites, docks, trails, picnic shelters and a paddle-landing site.

Mermaid Island

Situated four kilometres south of Gananoque, Mermaid Island is approximately a hectare and a half in size and another of the original park islands. There is no camping but there is a trail and a dock.

Beau Rivage Island

A few kilometres southwest of Gananoque is Beau Rivage Island. The approximately four-hectare island features red oak and a rocky shore. Lots of facilities and services are offered on the popular island including numerous campsites, docks, picnics shelters, a paddle-landing site as well as garbage and recycling. Beau Rivage is another of the park's original islands.

McDonald Island

Located about a kilometre offshore from Gananoque lies McDonald Island. Part of the island is privately owned with cottages while approximately 15 hectares, acquired in 1969, belongs to TINP. A rolling topography with deep soils, a deciduous forest and a marsh are featured on this island. A good

Tour boats are popular in the Thousand Islands area

Signs for trails at Landon Bay

selection of facilities and services are offered here including numerous campsites, trails, docks, garbage and recycling as well as a paddle-landing site. McDonald Island offers oTENTik accommodations.

Thwartway Island

This island lies a few kilometres from Gananoque and is the largest island entirely owned by TINP. The 40-hectare island was acquired in 1971. While Thwartway does not have docks or campsites, it does have mooring buoys and a paddle-landing site. It also features a natural sand beach, a rarity in the Thousand Islands area, which is popular with swimmers.

Numerous species of birds, amphibians, reptiles and plants live in the forests and wetlands of this island. Several at-risk plant species can also be found here. Part of the island was farmed in the past. Thwartway was the site of a military convalescent hospital for Canadian soldiers during World War I and some of the old ruins from this time can still be seen.

Camelot Island

Another of the park's original islands, Camelot Island is over nine hectares in size and is situated about five kilometres southeast of Gananoque. The popular island is rugged with considerable bare rock and some rare plant species. Docks, mooring buoys, a paddle-landing site and campsites are some of the facilities found here.

Endymion Island

Just east of Camelot Island is Endymion Island. This island is another of the original park properties and is a little more than four hectares in size. Consisting of a narrow granite ridge, Endymion has white pine, red and white oak and some rare plant species including the deerberry bush. Mooring buoys and docks are at this island.

Gordon Island

Gordon Island, situated approximately four kilometres east of Gananoque, is another of the park's original islands. While most of the islands in the TINP are granite, this six-hectare island is sandstone. The island boasts a good diversity of plant species including some rare species such as downy goldenrod. The island is also home to a significant mature red oak forest, the understory of which supports one of the densest carpets of spring ephemeral flowers in the park with colourful Dutchman's breeches making their appearance in April and May. Gordon Island is also a good spot for bird watchers during the spring migration. Archaeological sites on the island indicate that humans have lived in this area for thousands of years. Gordon Island is also home to one of the three gazebos that were originally built after 1904. The other gazebos are on Grenadier Island – West and at Mallorytown Landing. Some campsites and oTENTik accommodations along with a paddle-landing site, docking, picnic shelters and trails are some of the facilities found on Gordon Island.

Mulcaster Island

Located south of Landon Bay and approximately four kilometres west of Ivy Lea is Mulcaster Island. Acquired by the park in 1967, this island is more than five hectares in size. It has a good diversity of plant and tree species. Trails, a couple of campsites, a dock and a paddle-landing site are on the island.

Georgina Island

Georgina Island is situated just south of

oTENTik on Gordon Island

Ivy Lea and just north of Hill Island. It is nearly 10 hectares in size. Another of the park's original properties, this island sits underneath the Thousand Islands International Bridge. Trails, a couple of campsites, a paddle-landing site and docks can be found here.

Constance Island

Immediately south of Georgina Island and just north of Hill Island sits Constance Island. The Thousand Islands International Bridge also passes over this approximately three-hectare island which is another of the original park islands. There are no campsites on Constance Island but there are docks, a paddle-landing site and a picnic shelter.

Hill Island – Batterman's Point

Parks Canada owns more than 370 hectares of Hill Island, although there are only limited park facilities at Batterman's Point. Deciduous and coniferous forests along with marshes and other habitats are featured on this island which is also home to a great diversity of reptiles and amphibians, including the at-risk black ratsnake, as well as many at-risk plant species. A large ridge of pitch pine is also found here. Besides park land, Hill Island also includes some commercial and residential property.

At Batterman's point on Hill Island boaters will find a dock and a picnic shelter. The Wallis C. Bird Estate was purchased at this location in 1921. Known as "Limberlost" the mansion

Constance Island

Islets are important for birds such as these double-crested cormorants and herring gulls

and boathouse no longer exist, but a gazebo and a house (now used by the Canadian Coast Guard) remain.

Grenadier Island

Thousand Islands National Park owns much of Grenadier Island which extends almost from Rockport to Mallorytown Landing. Park facilities and services on Grenadier are divided into west, central, north and east sections. Grenadier Island – West has docks and features a gazebo constructed of granite field stone. The picnic shelter was built soon after the park was established in 1904. Grenadier Island – Central has numerous campsites, including a group camping site, along with picnic shelters and docks. Grenadier Island – North has a couple of campsites and a dock while Grenadier Island – East features a few campsites, docks and a paddle-landing site. All four areas of the island have trails.

A variety of habitats exist on Grenadier Island as well as an esker. Various at-risk species of plants, including deerberry and pitch pine, are found on the island which is also home to many amphibians and reptiles, including Blanding's turtles.

Adelaide Island

Off of the east end of Grenadier Island lies Adelaide Island. The approximately

Thousand Islands International Bridge

five-hectare island is another of the park's originals. This island features important habitat for water birds, amphibians and reptiles. It also has a high diversity of plants including some species at risk. A significant native archaeological site also exists here. While there are no campsites on Adelaide, there are several mooring buoys and a picnic shelter.

Stovin Island

Stovin Island is located just west of Brockville. Campsites are not available on this island but there are docks, picnic shelters and a paddle-landing site.

For more information: www.parkscanada.gc.ca/ti

OUR PARK ADVENTURES

Our first visit to Thousand Islands National Park occurred in early August. We arrived early in the afternoon and were given a pleasant boat tour of some of the park's islands by Parks Canada. We set off from Mallorytown Landing and our first destination was Georgina Island. Located just south of Ivy Lea, the beautiful island has a nice trail which took us through a coniferous forest along the edge of the island. There were wonderful views of other nearby islands and cottages on the St. Lawrence River. Tour boats were not uncommon and the Thousand Islands International Bridge is nearby. The west end of Georgina Island has undergone a prescribed burn which sat in sharp contrast to the rest of the island with its large coniferous trees. Some of the larger, burnt trees were still standing while others near the trail had been cut down for safety reasons. Bushes along with some young pine trees had already established themselves. Our walk soon took us back into the shade of the forest with the St. Lawrence River always nearby.

Next on our park tour was Gordon Island which is part of the Navy Islands. After docking we followed a scenic trail around the perimeter. Views of the river in all directions were spectacular. We set off on a trail where large oak trees and sumac grew. A large rock- and wood-columned gazebo caught our attention.

Georgina Island

Georgina Island

are the numerous islets, fascinating river landforms that provide important resting and nesting sites for birds, including double-crested cormorants. These incredible though much maligned birds were often in view as we toured the 30-kilometre stretch from Mallorytown Landing in the east to Gordon Island in the west.

We ended our day trip at Jones Creek, a short drive from Mallorytown Landing. There is a nice network of trails at Jones Creek and we hiked a few of the footpaths before driving home. It had been a very enjoyable day on the St. Lawrence River.

****

Built between 1904 and 1907, this shelter is one of three such structures that remain in the park.

Part of Gordon Island has also undergone a prescribed burn. The remains of burnt trees were still evident. Bushes were growing where the burns had cleared much of the former plant life.

Some trees on Gordon Island are very large. The big oaks are especially impressive. As we hiked the island we came across some tidy campsites. We also met two mink, one with a fish who didn't seem particularly concerned with our sudden appearance.

We later passed Mulcaster, Constance, Adelaide and Grenadier islands. Grenadier is a large island extending from near Rockport to Mallorytown Landing. Equally impressive

Our second visit to TINP was a strictly land-based excursion. It was a warm June day when we arrived. Our first destination was the Thousand Islands Tower. While this 130-metre-tall observation tower, located on Hill Island, isn't actually in the park, it does provide stunning views of Hill Island, 370 hectares of which are owned by the park as well as the Thouand Islands area.

Mallorytown Landing was our next stop where we got the added attraction of seeing the "Aboriginal Day Celebration." This annual event celebrates the close relationship between TINP and the Mohawks of Akwesasne who co-operate on numerous park projects and also consider this area traditional land. Scattered throughout the grounds were beautiful Mohawk rock carvings. These carvings represent the elements of creation and form part of a Thanksgiving Address greeting. This greeting, also known as "The Words That Come Before All Else," is at the core of the Haudenosaunee Confederacy's (of which the Mohawks of Akwesasne are a part) view of the universe. Associated symbols are also found on a nearby "Contemplation Rock" next to the St. Lawrence River.

We also checked out the waterfront gazebo made of granite field stone, one of three such gazebos in the park. We then checked out the boat launch area and the awesome oTENTiks before heading to our next stop – Landon Bay.

Landon Bay is located west of Mallorytown Landing between Ivy Lea and Gananoque. Scenic trails wind their way through mature forests. After passing through a medieval-looking stone archway we entered a beautiful deciduous forest. Our destination was a lookout.

To reach our goal, we navigated a section of the Donevan Trail and then took the Lookout Trail which ended in a breath-taking lookout perched high above Landon Bay and providing an excellent south-easterly view of the St. Lawrence and the Thousand Islands. While much of the hike was easy-going, there were

Boat launch area at Mallorytown Landing

some relatively steep sections as well as areas of the path where you had to navigate some rocks. A bench provided a place to rest and relax as we enjoyed the view. Be careful here, especially if you have children or a canine companion with you, as it is a long way down!

Our hike back to the car was also enjoyable – and not just because we were going downhill. We observed a surprising number of animals as well, including a gartersnake crossing the path in front of us. The forest was incredible and included shagbark hickory along with a variety of dazzling wildflowers.

After a little more than an hour in the verdant woods we decided to head home. What a fun day and a good way to get an appreciation of Thousand Islands National Park's mainland properties.

Gazebo at Mallorytown Landing

Rocky bluff on Grenadier Island

Nature plays an important role in the health of children

8. HEALTHY ENCOUNTERS: NATURE'S MANY BENEFITS

"Climb the mountains and get their good tidings. Nature's peace will flow into you as the sunshine into the trees. The winds will blow their freshness into you, and the storms their energy, while cares will drop off like autumn leaves." – John Muir

John Muir knew about the health benefits of Mother Nature, even though he wasn't a doctor. Muir was a naturalist, founder of the Sierra Club and a pioneer of the conservation movement who lived from 1838 – 1914. The environmental activist was instrumental in the creation of Yosemite National Park and was involved in the establishing of several other national parks in the United States. Muir spent time in Canada as well, including working at a sawmill near Meaford, Ontario from 1864 to 1866.

In addition to the quotation above, Muir has other fine examples where he credits nature's ability to heal and restore.

"Take a course in good water and air; and in the eternal youth of Nature you may renew your own. Go quietly, alone; no harm will befall you."

Or on the healing powers of nature and the importance of having wilderness accessible to people.

"Everybody needs beauty as well as bread, places to play in and pray in, where nature may heal and give strength to body and soul."

NATURE & HEALING IN THE LATE 19TH CENTURY

Nineteenth-century doctors also observed that nature and fresh air could heal, prescribing time in a natural setting for some of their patients affected by respiratory issues. One thought was that the smell of evergreen trees was good for the lungs.

One place where people suffering from a variety of health issues went to heal was Algonquin Park. In her book *Algonquin Park's Mowat: Little Town of Big Dreams*, Mary I. Garland discusses nature's role in healing during the early 1900s.

"The new century had ushered in new thinking about health. People were starting to believe that outdoor living, particularly the scent of pine trees, was beneficial for many ailments, and they started spending time away from cities in more natural surroundings. There was definite validity to the benefits of outdoor living away from urban areas, but for reasons not yet understood at the time. People who could afford to escape city life in the hot summer did so, and the wilderness of Algonquin Park beckoned."

Garland states that hotels, such as the Algonquin Hotel and the Highland Inn, in Algonquin Park publicized the health benefits of a stay in the park.

"Both these hotels advertised the benefit to overall health, although the Highland Inn would not accept tuberculosis patients, leaving a niche for other lodges to fill during an era when both tuberculosis and exposure to poisonous gas from World War I were taking their toll on people."

CHILDREN & YOUNG ADULTS SUFFERING FROM STRESS & OTHER ILLS

In recent years a drove of reports, surveys and articles have focused on the psychological distress suffered by students and teenagers. In fact, the problem of mental illness with children and young adults has been described as a "crisis." They are suffering from stress, anxiety and depression at alarming rates. There are various reasons for these serious mental health issues, including the pressures of doing well in school, college and university.

While teenagers and post-secondary students are suffering from mental health issues, young children are also affected. In the article "The Whole Child: A Pediatrician Recommends the Nature Prescription," author Lawrence Rosen, MD, lists many of the health problems children are suffering from today.

"Kids are being diagnosed with anxiety, depression, ADHD, irritable bowel syndrome and migraine headaches at all-time high rates. Whatever labels we want to use, the message is clear – our children are suffering from stress."

How do we deal with mental health issues affecting children? While there are various ways to address children suffering from things

Hiking in nature has many benefits

like stress, depression and anxiety, the positive results achieved by getting them into nature cannot be ignored. Dr. Rosen goes on to state the importance of nature to a child's health.

"Getting kids back into nature is a key part of the solution to keeping kids healthy and truly creating wellness. A mounting number of research studies highlight the positive impact of free outdoor play on children's emotional and physical health."

Richard Louv links many of the consequences of children being disconnected from nature – consequences that include attention difficulties and higher rates of physical and emotional illnesses - in his ground-breaking book *Last Child in the Woods: Saving Our Children from Nature-Deficit Disorder*. According to Louv, direct exposure to nature is important for healthy childhood development – physical, emotional and spiritual.

One organization in Ontario working to connect children and families with regular, meaningful nature experiences is the Back to Nature Network. This group of organizations believes that daily access to nature is essential for the intellectual, physical, and emotional well-being of children and works collaboratively in many ways to achieve this goal.

It is not just children, teenagers and young adults who are suffering from mental health issues, adults are too. The good news is that nature, trees and green spaces have numerous health benefits including reducing stress and depression and improving our ability

Kayaking in Point Pelee National Park

There are health benefits associated with being near water

to concentrate. Nature can also help those with attention deficit hyperactivity disorder (ADHD).

ENJOY NATURE WITHOUT THE SCREENS

Nature can also contribute to our well-being by minimizing things that can make us ill. Outdoor pursuits like hiking trails, canoeing lakes, camping and bird watching have mental and physical health benefits. When we are engaging in these fun, healthy activities, we are not spending time (or at least the time is significantly reduced) looking at a screen, playing video games, surfing the internet or texting people. The dramatic increase in the amount of time spent in front of screens during the last few decades has resulted in serious widespread health issues. Some such ailments include ADHD, anxiety, depression, addiction and increased aggression.[16]

Fortunately, these psychological problems can often be effectively dealt with when we significantly reduce screen time (and possibly temporarily eliminate screen time with a digital timeout) and obtain healing by reconnecting with the natural world.

NATURE HELPS WITH PHYSICAL HEALING

Mother Nature not only helps with numerous mental health issues, but has proven helpful with our physical health as well.

Harebells

A much-cited study by Roger S. Ulrich pertains to patients in a Pennsylvania hospital from 1972 to 1981 who had surgery to remove their gallbladders. The patients recovered in one of two areas of the hospital. One side of the hospital featured windows with a view of a small forest while the other looked at bricks. The study found that patients who had a view of trees had shorter post-operative hospital stays, used fewer moderate and strong medications for pain and had fewer complaints.

THE HEALTH BENEFITS OF FOREST BATHING

The belief by some medical professionals in the late 19th century that the scent of evergreen trees was good for you has been strongly supported by recent studies including those done by Dr. Qing Li on the Japanese practice of forest bathing. Shinrin-yoku, Japanese for "forest bathing," involves a leisurely walk in a forest which is shown to lower blood pressure and decrease stress, anxiety, depression and anger. Forest bathing also appears to help our immune system while fighting off cancer. Some of the benefits of forest bathing are obtained from breathing in air containing phytoncides (wood essential oils) given off by the trees.

NATURE HELPS LEARNING, TEACHING & ACADEMIC PERFORMANCE

When it comes to schools and teaching, nature proves a boon again. The report "Nature Nurtures: Investigating the Potential of School Grounds," published by the organization Evergreen, focuses on the positive aspects of nature-oriented school grounds. Two positive results of transforming school grounds into more natural environments are improved academic performances of students, and increased teacher enthusiasm.

Another study that illustrates the positive effects that nature has on students is "High School Landscapes and Student Performance" by Dr. Rodney H. Matsuoka. Dr. Matsuoka found that nature, including views of it, have positive effects on the academic performance and behaviour of high school students.

PROXIMITY TO WATER PROVIDES HEALTH BENEFITS

While considerable research has been conducted on how forests, parks and other green spaces are good for us, there isn't as much information regarding the health benefits of being near water. I always feel better when I look out over a lake, hike near a river or stream or spend time observing wildlife in and around a wetland. Almost immediately I begin to relax and feel better. This feeling is explained in Wallace J. Nichols' book *Blue Mind: The Surprising Science That Shows How Being Near, In, On, or Under Water Can Make You Happier, Healthier, More Connected, and Better at What You Do.*

NATURE ENCOURAGES EXERCISE

For much of society, physical fitness has declined while obesity has risen, causing a variety of health problems. Fortunately, spending time in nature usually involves hiking and other forms of exercise. This exercise helps prevent heart disease, lower cholesterol, control and prevent diabetes, reduce obesity, lower blood pressure and help with arthritis and osteoporosis.

These physical benefits, combined with the psychological advantages of nature, are good reasons to strap on the hiking boots. And this fact hasn't gone unnoticed by the medical community. In the United States there is even a "Parks Prescriptions" program. This initiative sees the National Park Service work with health care professionals to provide appropriate prescriptions to walk, bicycle, paddle or do some other appropriate exercise in nature. This concept linking the medical community and their patients to exercise in a natural setting is a progressive move and, hopefully, one that can become firmly implanted in our future health care systems.

In Ontario, programs encouraging people to exercise in nature are making headway. One such initiative is "Mood Walks." These walks are a provincial initiative of the Canadian Mental Health Association, Ontario in partnership with Hike Ontario and Conservation Ontario. They promote physical and mental health through group walks on local hiking trails and at conservation areas.

SHEDDING LIGHT ON THE IMPORTANCE OF DARK SKIES

Keeping skies dark at night is not just vital for wildlife, it is also important for humans. Artificial light at night affects ecosystems and can have devastating consequences for birds, mammals, amphibians, reptiles and insects.

Our species is also suffering. And there aren't many places left on the planet where you can go to experience a night similar to what our ancestors did. This is tragic, not only because we are losing the beauty of the night skies, but also because light pollution negatively affects our own health. In *The End of Night: Searching for Natural Darkness in an Age of Artificial Light*, author Paul Bogard shows how artificial light at night disrupts our sleep, suppresses melatonin production and negatively impacts our circadian rhythms (biological clocks). These impacts can lead to a variety of health issues.

Efforts to minimize such artificial light will help ensure the health of humans and other animals.

Enjoying the many wonders of nature can help relieve stress and anxiety

A beautiful view of Cyprus Lake's clear waters

PARK ETIQUETTE, SAFETY & MINIMAL FOOTPRINTS

"We have forgotten how to be good guests, how to walk lightly on the earth as its other creatures do."
– Barbara Ward

Enjoying the national parks safely and without impacting on them is easily accomplished if you use common sense, follow some rules and are a considerate guest in these wilderness areas. The intent of this section is not to list all the things you should do while enjoying a national park, but rather to leave you with a general philosophy that it is a privilege to be in a revered nature area and also, to provide some tips on how to safely enjoy your stays there.

YOU'RE IN SOMEONE ELSE'S HOME...ACT LIKE IT!

While enjoying the national parks and the incredible wilderness that they protect, we must remember that we are only visitors here. These parks are the homes to thousands of species of plants and animals and as long as we remember that and act as well-mannered guests should, we will not make many mistakes. The following are some things that we should keep in mind while staying in a national park.

LAWS, REGULATIONS & RULES

All rules, regulations and laws pertaining to national parks must be followed. Take the time to find out what permits, if any, you will need for your visit along with laws, regulations and rules associated with things like camping, boating, campfires, hiking, pets, noise and wildlife. Learning this park information in advance may save you disappointment later. Some offences in national parks carry heavy fines and could result in jail time. If you witness someone who might be committing an offence, report the incident to a park employee. For more information visit: www.pc.gc.ca/acts

TRAIL ETIQUETTE

When hiking the trails make sure you stay on marked footpaths. By keeping on the trail you will greatly minimize damage to plants and the environment. If you are part of a group, walk in single-file so that others using the trail have room to pass along the trail.

If you are hiking with a canine companion, ensure that your dog is allowed along that path. Your "best friend" should be on a leash, fit enough to accompany you on a hike, have appropriate identification and is up-to-date with vaccinations. Since your dog is likely to meet others on the trail, she should be expected to be friendly to both people and other dogs. Depending on the length of your hike, you should consider taking along some water, snacks and first-aid items for your four-legged family member. Make sure your dog also keeps to the trails and is not allowed to frighten animals.

OBSERVE, DON'T TAKE – OR MOVE

Enjoy the scenery, but leave things where they are. It is illegal to collect or remove plants, animals, animal parts such as antlers, artifacts, fossils, rocks and other natural objects in the park. These are part of the park ecosystem and serve a purpose. They are protected by law and must be left undisturbed. If you think you have found something significant, leave the item where it is and report your find to a park employee. Refrain from moving objects as well. Do not collect deadfall for fires or stack rocks into cairns. Stay on the trails and observe the beauty of the park from there and leave everything else in its natural place.

OBSERVE WILDLIFE... FROM A SAFE DISTANCE

Wildlife viewing can be a significant part of your national park experience. Observing animals in their environment is an experience that you won't soon forget. Don't, however, put your safety or the safety of animals at risk. Every year well-meaning people put themselves in jeopardy as well as the lives of animals when they get too close. It is illegal to pursue, feed, harass or pet wild animals in a national park.

Feeding wild animals is a bad idea for many reasons. Not only are you altering their diet or possibly giving them something that could make them sick, but the animals might later approach other people for food. This behaviour can cause problems and possibly put the animal's life in jeopardy.

Do not approach wild animals. Respect them by giving them their space and admire them from a distance.

PHOTOGRAPHY

Taking photographs is a good way to capture the beauty of the natural world and to preserve memories of your visit. When taking photographs step to the side of the trail so you aren't in the way of others. If you are taking photographs at a popular spot, take a few photos and then step aside so that others can also capture the view with their cameras.

Never disturb or frighten animals when taking photographs. Since you have to stay on the trails, you might want to use a zoom lens when photographing wildlife. Do not use a flash. Just as you don't appreciate your photo taken with a flash, animals don't either.

NOISE

National parks are places where people go to enjoy the beauty and solitude of nature, not hear excessive noise from others. Enjoy the park, but be considerate of other visitors as well as park residents.

GARBAGE

The best thing that you can do regarding your garbage is create as little as you can. Use reusable containers to transport food and other items whenever possible. Recycle what you can and follow a "pack in, pack out" policy where you take your garbage with you when your visit is over.

ITEMS TO CONSIDER TAKING

What you take on your park adventures depends on a variety of things including where you are going, the length of stay and what you plan on doing when you get there. The following are some items you should consider packing for your park visit, even if you are only going for the day.

Clothes should be comfortable. Depending on the weather you might want to dress in layers so you can add or remove layers as necessary. You will want to wear quality hiking boots or shoes with a good tread or, at the very least, a durable pair of running shoes. A second pair of socks is also a good idea. If rain is in the forecast, you might take along a lightweight, folding umbrella and rainwear. Any equipment, such as cameras, should also be adequately protected from the elements.

Take plenty of drinking water as it is important to stay hydrated. Other recommended items include nutritious snacks, first-aid kit, emergency whistle, cell phone, flashlight, compass and/or GPS, map, pocketknife, and fire starters (matches or lighter).

Protection from the sun is also important so consider taking a wide brimmed hat, sunglasses, sunscreen and clothing that provides sun protection.

SAFETY

National parks are special places to visit, but it is important to keep safe while you enjoy your wilderness outing. It is a good idea to let others know where you are going, when you are leaving and when you plan to return. This is particularly important if you go alone.

Wear appropriate clothes and footwear. You want to be both comfortable and protected while hiking trails, camping and enjoying various other activities in the park. Sandals aren't appropriate for hiking many trails or walking in rocky, and other rugged, areas.

If you are in a park where bears live, learn about precautions you should take in case you encounter some of these fascinating animals. Give them their space and an escape route. Try to avoid sudden encounters or surprising a bear. If possible, travel in groups and make noise. Be aware of your surroundings. When camping, make sure that your food is properly stored away and inaccessible to animals. Report any incidents to park staff.

Protect yourself from ticks. The blacklegged tick can spread Lyme disease through its bite. Wearing a long-sleeved shirt as well as pants tucked into your socks will reduce your chances of tick bites. Wearing light-coloured clothing is also a good idea as you can better see ticks on these clothes. Take the time to regularly inspect yourself and other members of your family, including children and pets.

Part of the reason why the national parks in this book are so special is because they feature a variety of habitats along with scenic, rugged places. While young children and pets should always be supervised, they need to be especially protected near lookouts, cliffs, water and other dangerous sites. Pets should be on a leash and children should be educated about the dangers of these sites and the importance of staying on marked trails.

Watching the weather and checking weather forecasts is another way to help ensure your safety. Check the weather in advance and keep heed of changing weather and approaching storms along the way. This will give you a head start in seeking effective shelter.

Park employees are there to help, so don't hesitate to ask them about a variety of concerns including updates on weather, potential hazards and any unknown risks in the park. Take the time to let them know of any incidents, or potential incidents, that you encountered as this can help improve park safety.

Finally, make sure that you, and those in your group, are able to safely accomplish the activities that you undertake. If you are older, or not in good shape, first check with your doctor as to how much you can do. The parks in this book contain a variety of trails from easy to difficult. Select the trails that are suitable for you, and those you might be hiking with as well.

You should also be experienced enough to do the activities that you select. If you are canoeing or kayaking, make sure that you can safely handle the conditions you will likely encounter. Take along all required boat safety equipment and always wear a lifejacket or personal flotation device.

Enjoying a quiet moment on Flowerpot Island

9. A FINAL WORD

"We must realize that all life is valuable and that we are united to all life. From this knowledge comes our spiritual relationship with the universe." – Albert Schweitzer

During the last decade my wife Lynn and I and, to a lesser extent, our children Gleannan and Liam, have made numerous excursions into Southern Ontario's national parks. Every visit to these wilderness areas has been special. The scenery is spectacular, the trails are well-maintained and there is lots to see and do. These parks provide the public with access to some of the most scenic wilderness in the province. Both terrestrial and aquatic habitats can be found in all of the parks.

Whether you are enjoying the waters of Georgian Bay, the St Lawrence River or Lake Huron, exploring the marsh and beaches at Point Pelee, hiking the extensive forests and scenic coastlines of the Bruce Peninsula or experiencing the variety of habitats in Canada's first national urban park, your visit will be time well spent. Not only will you enjoy pristine wilderness that these parks are protecting, you will also receive health benefits.

Spending time in nature has been shown to have a variety of health advantages including both physical and psychological benefits. People, particularly children, who have been exposed to too much screen time also profit from spending time in nature – without their electronic devices (or limited use if a total ban

Wetlands on Beausoleil Island, Georgian Bay Islands National Park

isn't an option). I always feel more relaxed and refreshed after spending time in a park, even if it is only for a few hours.

While our national parks are important from a recreational perspective, their greatest value lies in protecting some of the best wilderness left in this increasingly urbanized part of the province. As subdivisions, roads, shopping centres and other development continues to fragment natural habitat into increasingly smaller pieces, it is essential to preserve those wilderness areas that remain. Connecting the parks to other green spaces is also important in protecting the area's biodiversity.

While good examples of wilderness, Southern Ontario's national parks are isolated islands in a sea of urban and agricultural development. Across the continent biodiversity and animal populations are declining. Here in Ontario, bats, birds and amphibians are some animals facing serious threats including habitat loss and degradation.

An effective way to ensure species survival and a healthy environment involves not only setting aside and protecting more natural habitat, but connecting these parks, trails and other green spaces via nature corridors. An unfragmented network of nature corridors, connecting wilderness islands of various sizes, would result in increased species immigration between areas, less inbreeding, larger populations, more foraging areas and shelter and increased species diversity. This

Hiking in Bruce Peninsula National Park

wilderness network would also reduce the impacts on climate change and it would be a model of how people can live more sustainably in urban areas while co-existing with other species. Such a network would be an incredible legacy to leave all of the species of Southern Ontario – and beyond!

Unfortunately, while levels of government often claim that a healthy environment and biodiversity are important, they do little to control urban development and encourage sustainable living. Gone are the magnificent forests that once covered Southern Ontario. The vast majority of pre-settlement wetlands here have also been destroyed adversely affecting biodiversity, water quality, and flood control and contributing to global warming. Forests, meadows and other habitats are also under attack in the name of "progress" (which is anything but).

On a more positive note, during our park visits Lynn and I enjoyed exploring some relatively recent land acquisitions in some of the parks. It was reassuring to see some of the national parks getting larger. Increasing the size of national parks would improve the "ecological integrity" of the parks and these goals should be a priority for Parks Canada.

New land acquisitions will not only enlarge an existing national park, they can also provide a buffer area around the park where wildlife can live and travel while being protected. Just as cities and towns expand from a central area, parks should be encouraged to grow as properties become available. Educating property owners near parks about keeping their land in a natural state – and even providing incentives for responsible land stewardship – would also increase suitable habitat.

I was also encouraged to see that three of the national parks in Southern Ontario have been designated Dark-Sky Preserves. Artificial light at night negatively impacts wildlife (and humans) in numerous ways. Protecting the parks not only involves protecting the plants and animals who reside there, but also the habitats and resources. Preserving the night sky in and around the parks is a vital resource to protect and an important goal for our national parks.

In Southern Ontario we don't have to travel too far to reach a national park and enjoy its incredible beauty – and get a glimpse of what our ancestors saw many years ago. Gathering the family together, even for a day trip, in a national park will result in a fun time and create wonderful memories. Of course, a longer stay will likely be even more special.

This close proximity to national parks in the most populated part of the country will place considerable pressure on these wilderness areas. As more people travel to the parks to enjoy a wilderness experience – and receive the health benefits from Mother Nature – large numbers will detract from the secluded, back-to-nature feeling many of us desire.

Milky way over the Bruce Peninsula Photo: © Gabriel Guillén

Although we didn't experience many crowded situations in the parks, there were a few occasions in the summer where an event or a popular site did attract lots of people. Concerns with increased tourism demands with some of the parks, particularly with some popular spots in the parks, have been raised.

One way to both increase park attendance while helping to ensure that overcrowding is minimized is to encourage more visitors to experience the parks outside of the busy summer months. Lynn and I had one of our most enjoyable park visits when we hiked some trails in Bruce Peninsula National Park during the winter. We walked to some of the most popular areas in the park and only saw about a dozen people. We have also experienced the beautiful fall colours in several of the parks and on each of these occasions attendance in the parks was not high.

As our species continues its assault on the natural world, it is somewhat comforting to know that there are still some relatively pristine pockets of wilderness left in Southern Ontario that we can visit. These national parks are ideal places for a relaxing get-away where you can get energized while enjoying the spectacular scenery, fascinating wildlife and a variety of activities. Whether a day trip or a longer vacation, such a visit will generate fond memories spent in a special place.

The rugged beauty of Bruce Peninsula National Park

ENDNOTES

1. Bob Day, *Shores of Heaven: the birth of Bruce Peninsula National Parks* (2012)
2. S. Parker and M. Munawar editors, *Ecology, Culture and Conservation of a Protected Area: Fathom Five National Marine Park, Canada* (Leiden: Backhuys Publishers, 2001).
3. Peter E. Kelly & Douglas W. Larson, *The Last Stand: A Journey Through the Ancient Cliff-Face Forest of the Niagara Escarpment* (Toronto: Natural Heritage Books, 2007).
4. S. Parker and M. Munawar editors, *Ecology, Culture and Conservation of a Protected Area: Fathom Five National Marine Park, Canada* (Leiden: Backhuys Publishers, 2001).
5. Ibid.
6. Peter E. Kelly and Douglas W. Larson, *The Last Stand: A Journey Through the Ancient Cliff-Face Forest of the Niagara Escarpment* (Toronto: Natural Heritage Books, 2007).
7. Kevin McNamee, *The National Parks of Canada* (Toronto: Key Porter Books, 1994).
8. Su Murdoch editor, *A Taste of Honey Harbour: The Area and Its People* (Honey Harbour: Honey Harbour Historical Committee, 1999).
9. Darryl Stewart, *Point Pelee: Canada's Deep South* (Toronto: Burns and MacEachern Limited, 1977).
10. Ibid.
11. Tammy Dobbie, Trevor McFadyen, Paul Zorn, Josh Keitel, Terra Ecological Consulting (Matt Carlson), "Point Pelee National Park of Canada State of the Park Report 2006", Parks Canada, 2007.
12. Ibid.
13. Ibid.
14. Ibid.
15. Henrietta T. O'Neill, *Birding at Point Pelee* (Toronto: James Lorimer & Company Ltd., Publishers, 2006).
16. Nicholas Kardaras, *Glow Kids: How Screen Addiction is Hijacking Our Kids – and How to Break the Trance* (New York: St. Martin's Press, 2016).

Cyprus Lake, Bruce Peninsula National Park

SELECT BIBLIOGRAPHY

The following books were both interesting and useful in the writing of this book.

1. Bogard, Paul. *The End of Night: Searching for Natural Darkness in an Age of Artificial Light.* New York: Little, Brown and Company, 2013.
2. Burtch, Kathleen, comp. *Life on the Edge: The Cultural Landscape of the Thousand Islands Area.* Gananoque: Canadian Thousand Islands Heritage Conservancy, 2004.
3. Day, Bob. *Shores of Heaven: the birth of Bruce Peninsula National Parks.* 2013.
4. Eyles, Nick. *Road Rocks Ontario: Over 250 Geological Wonders to Discover.* Markham: Fitzhenry & Whiteside, 2013.
5. Fox, W. Sherwood. *The Bruce Beckons: The Story of Lake Huron's Great Peninsula* (Revised and Enlarged Edition). Toronto: University of Toronto Press, 2002.
6. Francis, George. *Striving for Environmental Sustainability in a Complex World: Canadian Experiences.* Vancouver: UBC Press, 2016.
7. Garratt, James E. *The Rouge River Valley: An Urban Wilderness.* Toronto: Natural Heritage Books, 2000.
8. Kardaras, Nicholas. *Glow Kids: How Screen Addiction is Hijacking Our Kids – and How to Break the Trance.* New York: St. Martin's Press, 2016.
9. Kelly, Peter E. and Douglas W. Larson. *The Last Stand: A Journey Through the Ancient Cliff-Face Forest of the Niagara Escarpment.* Toronto: Natural Heritage Books, 2007.
10. Lothian, W.F. *A Brief History of Canada's National Parks.* Environment Canada, Parks, 1987.
11. Louv, Richard. *Last Child in the Woods: Saving Our Children from Nature-Deficit Disorder* (Updated and Expanded). Chapel Hill: Algonquin Books of Chapel Hill, 2008.
12. Louv, Richard. *The Nature Principle: Reconnecting with Life in a Virtual Age.* Chapel Hill: Algonquin Books of Chapel Hill, 2012.
13. McIlwraith, Thomas F., ed *The Land Between: Encounters on the Edge of the Canadian Shield.* Markham: Fitzhenry & Whiteside, 2013.

14. McNamee, Kevin. *The National Parks of Canada.* Toronto: Key Porter Books Limited, 1994.
15. Nichols, Wallace J. *Blue Mind: the Surprising Science That Shows How Being Near, In, On, or Under Water Can Make You Happier, Healthier, More Connected, and Better at What You Do.* New York: Little, Brown and Company, 2014.
16. O'Neill, Henrietta. *In Search of a Heart.* Friends of Point Pelee, 2000.
17. O'Neill, Henrietta T. *Birding at Point Pelee: A Birder's History of One of Canada's Most Famous Birding Spots.* Toronto: James Lorimer & Company Ltd., 2006.
18. Parker, S. and Munawar, M. eds. *Ecology, Culture and Conservation of a Protected Area: Fathom Five National Marine Park, Canada.* Leiden: Backhuys Publishers, 2001.
19. Robins, Cathy, ed *Hewers of the Forests Fishers of the Lakes: A History of Tobermory and St. Edmunds Township 1870 – 1984* (2nd Edition, Revised). Tobermory: Tobermory Press Inc., 2010.
20. Ross, Don. *St. Lawrence Islands National Park.* Vancouver: Douglas & McIntyre, 1983.
21. Selhub, Eva M. and Alan C. Logan. *Your Brain on Nature: The Science of Nature's Influence on Your Health, Happiness, and Vitality.* Mississauga: John Wiley & Sons Canada, Ltd., 2012.
22. Stewart, Darryl. *Point Pelee: Canada's Deep South.* Don Mills: Burns and MacEachern Limited, 1977.
23. Thompson, Ken. *Where Do Camels Belong?: The Story and Science of Invasive Species.* Vancouver: Greystone Books, 2014.
24. Tovell, Walter M. *Guide to the Geology of the Niagara Escarpment.* The Niagara Escarpment Commission, 1992.
25. Wright, Larry and Patricia. *Great Lakes Lighthouses Encyclopedia.* Richmond Hill: The Boston Mills Press, 2011.

ACKNOWLEDGEMENTS

Creating a book of this nature is not easily accomplished without the help of others. First and foremost I want to thank my wife, and best friend, Lynn. This book would not have occurred without Lynn whose enthusiasm in visiting the parks, time and patience in reading the manuscript and offering suggestions and taking and selecting photographs for the book were invaluable. Many of the best photographs in the book were taken by Lynn.

Our children, Gleannan and Liam, were also important in the book's creation. Their enjoyment of the natural world is inspirational and a reminder that we need more, not less, wilderness. Liam and Gleannan also accompanied us on some park visits, most notably to Georgian Bay Islands National Park. Gleannan also joined us on visits to Rouge National Urban Park, contributed photographs for the book and reviewed some of the chapters.

My parents, Helen and Norman, also played a key role in this book as they provided me (and my brothers) with easy access to wilderness while growing up in Sarnia and Thornhill as well as at our cottage on Georgian Bay. This opportunity to easily immerse myself in nature was instrumental in my respect for, and love of, the natural world. I would also like to thank my brothers, Keith and Neil, for their encouragement and support (yes Keith, the sidebars idea was a good one.)

Thanks are also extended to my parents-in-law, Audrey and Bob, for raising a wonderful daughter who loves nature and animals.

I would also like to acknowledge assistance from those with Parks Canada who graciously showed Lynn and I the parks, answered our questions, checked the chapters for accuracy and generally supported this book in a variety of ways. There are too many people from Parks Canada who assisted in some way to list here, but the efforts of the following people from Parks Canada were particularly helpful: Andrew Promaine, Jeffrey Sinibaldi, Sarah Rupert, Dan Simard, Scott Parker, Sheldon Lambert, Guy Thériault, Scott Sutton, Tina Jansen van Vuuren, Claire LaCroix, Suzanne Lambert, Sophie Borcoman.

Assistance from companies is always appreciated and I would like to thank the

Alchemist Canoe Company, Lee Valley, Grey Owl Paddles Limited and Coleman Canada for their support.

Others who provided much appreciated assistance include Chris Earley, Rob Laidlaw, Don Ross, Bill Kilburn, Randy Attwood, Kim Peters, Georgian Bay Biosphere Reserve, Frontenac Arch Biosphere Reserve, Bruce Trail Conservancy.

I would like to acknowledge the following for allowing me to quote information from their books: Friends of Point Pelee, Henrietta O'Neill, Thousand Islands Watershed Land Trust, Kathleen Burtch, Tobermory Press Inc., University of Toronto Press, Children & Nature Network, Dr. Lawrence Rosen, The Friends of Algonquin Park, Mary I. Garland, Firefly Books Ltd., Niagara Escarpment Commission, Douglas & McIntyre (2013) Ltd., Fitzhenry & Whiteside Publishing, Parks Canada.

Thanks also to Kerry Plumley for his efforts in designing this book.

Finally, I would like to thank everyone at Fitzhenry & Whiteside Publishing, particularly Sharon, Sonya and Peter who supported this project from the beginning.

Photo: © Gleannan Perrett

ABOUT THE AUTHOR

N. Glenn Perrett is a writer and environmentalist who lives with his family in Mulmur, Ontario. Glenn grew up in Southern Ontario in Sarnia and Thornhill and spent cherished summers at the family cottage on Georgian Bay. Canoeing, hiking, walking the dogs and spending time in nature are some of the author's favourite ways to spend a day. His interests include protecting animals and the environment and living lightly on Earth and these beliefs are reflected in Southern Ontario's National Parks – Glenn's third book.

DISCLAIMER

The information in this book is true to the best of the author's knowledge at the time of writing (2017). Recommendations are made without guarantee on the part of the author or Fitzhenry & Whiteside. The author and publisher disclaim any liability in connection with the use of this information. Outdoor activities, particularly those in the wilderness and on watercourses, bring an element of risk and danger. Trail conditions, and even trails, change. The reader should be aware of the current conditions (including weather) and possible hazards and knowledgeable that his/her skills and fitness level are appropriate for the activities and areas chosen.